Final Rose

Shawntel Newton

Memoir
BOOKS
Chico, CA

Final Rose

Copyright © 2012 by J. Shawntel Newton
Cover and title page photos by Amy Waltz

ISBN: 978-1-937748-00-5
Library of Congress Control Number 2012931086
First Edition

Memoir Books
An Imprint of Heidelberg Graphics
2 Stansbury Court
Chico, California 95928

Contents

This book is dedicated to my loving parents

Ric and Colene prior to their marriage, 1984

Acknowledgements

First and foremost, thank you Lord for all your blessings and most importantly … thank you for the patience you provided me to get this book done.

I want to say that I could not have done this book without the love and support from my family. Mom, you always believed in me and encouraged me every step of the way. Dad, I look up to you more than you will ever know. Destiny, you are such a strong, courageous woman and I admire you for that. Vanessa, you have grown up into a beautiful, bright woman. I could not have asked for better sisters. Love you.

Thank you to my all my girlfriends who had to sacrifice their friendship with me because of my social seclusion to write this book. Cheers, ladies!

Thank you to Amy Waltz for her cover photo session, Chico Florist for the flowers we used, and Sandra Dier for doing my hair and makeup.

A big thank you to all my friends and fans on Facebook and Twitter. Everyone has continued to give support to me throughout this process and I would be crazy not to mention you all in my acknowledgements. So thank you!

Thank you to the boyfriends who have been in my life

through all the ups and downs.

I would also like to thank Larry Jackson, my publisher. Larry, you have really helped me during the months of hard work with this book. I thank you for your honesty and patience with me.

One more thank you to ... *you* as a reader. Thank you for taking the time to read my story.

Yellow House

You know the saying: "Don't judge a book by its cover?" Well, you may be wondering why there is a young woman in a cemetery pictured on the front of this book's cover. I'm glad it caught your attention. My name is Shawntel Newton and I am the girl on the cover; here is my story.

I was born and raised in a small northern California town, Chico, the City of Trees. Chico is known for Bidwell Park—one of the largest municipal parks in the U.S., Sierra Nevada Brewing Co.—the second largest craft brewery in the U.S., the Sacramento River, California State University, Chico, and Bidwell Mansion—home of Chico's founder, John Bidwell and his wife Annie.

The fall season is always my favorite time in this town. Thousands of trees turn bright red and yellow and it's breathtaking (if you visit, I suggest you drive down the Esplanade flanked by giant sycamores). These attractions bring many visitors. I would have to say, Chico has been a good place to grow up.

I am the oldest of three girls. Altogether we're six years apart. Those who are the oldest in your family may relate when I say I was the child who had to set the pace and was used by my parents as the "tester."

Shawntel and sister Destiny posing with roses in front of their yellow house

My sisters and I grew up in a cute yellow house that Mom decorated with love. We had a small pool in the backyard and lots of room to play and run. We spent a lot of time in the yard with our parents and the animals. My dad Ric was gone a lot because of work, but he always managed to come home during the day to swim with his girls in the backyard and give us piggyback rides. We went to church most every Sunday and prayed with our dad every night. At bedtime, my middle sister Destiny and I would yell from bed (we shared a room), "Daaaaaddddd time to say our prayers." Dad would come in and pray with us, then we'd ask him to get us water and tuck us in.

We mostly spent our time with my mom, Colene, because Dad worked so much. Mom was our stronghold; she made sure we girls were up and ready for the day, lunches were made, sports gear gathered, homework done, and extra Band-Aids were available in case we fell again on the playground. When it was nighttime, we girls were excited because that meant we got to hang out with Dad. We never really knew the extent our dad's work until we got older. However, while we were young, we knew Dad helped people in our small town during a really hard time in their lives. I will get more into that soon (I don't want to scare you away from this book too quickly).

Not only did we know Dad was going to be home to help us get ready for bed, but on weekends he would take us fishing, camping, and sometimes when he had to go out of town for work we'd be able to go with him.

Growing up, we didn't get to watch a lot of television; instead we had to get our homework done first, then we were encouraged to go out and play with the neighbors and be active. I'm talking cops/robbers, Rollerblading, bike riding, street hockey, swimming, and much more. Honestly; I have never played a video game in my life—not even Mario Bros.—to this day. Okay, okay, okay, … I have and do play Wii, but I don't count that as a video game.

I grew up attending one of the largest churches in Chico with my two younger sisters. We called it, "the golf ball church." It's in the shape of a gold half-dome and looks like an enlarged gold golf ball. A creek runs along the church. We would play in the water at church camps and have picnics. My family and I almost lived at the golf ball church. I remember times my dad would be ushering while my middle sister and I napped on the benches. They were an odd green color but *so* comfortable. There was an upstairs and of course my sisters and I would run up and down the stairs playing hide-and-seek. We were involved in the church choir, plays, camps, and even leadership. It was a great foundation for our family.

There was the memorable church play titled *Candy Cane Lane*. I badly wanted the leading role. I tried out but didn't get the part. Instead I got a one-liner. My parents video recorded the play and to this day we watch it for a good laugh. Those times of rehearsing church plays are when I started to gain small crushes on boys.

There's another part of my childhood I want to share with you: not only did I grow up in the church with my family, but I also grew up in a funeral home. Yes, you read that right; I grew up in the business of death.

My Girl

LET ME CONTINUE by asking, have you seen the movie, *My Girl*? It's about a little girl who grows up with her dad who owns and operates his own funeral home, and the funeral home is their house. She was a hypochondriac and one of her best friend dies from bee stings. The movie shows her journey not only through grief but life in the funeral industry. Well … I am *not* a hypochondriac, but I, too, grew up with a dad who is a funeral director and embalmer. Mine was not your average childhood. We did things a little differently than most families.

Since living with a funeral director and embalmer was "normal" for our family, it didn't bother us but it did some others. Being young, my sisters and I remember that in the middle of the night Dad sometimes left and helped families. My sisters and I would wake up when we heard the garage door opening, knowing Dad was going to the funeral home to work. I don't think either of us went back to sleep until we heard the garage door reopen and we knew he was safely home.

SOMETIMES DAD BROUGHT me with him to the funeral home. As he was getting someone ready in the casket, Dad told me later, I would wonder, "Daddy, who's in the box?" I raised my arms for him to lift me to see who it was. Even as a little child I was curious, like most people are, about who is in the casket and what they look like. Dad recalled us daughters asking what their names were and why are they in the box? He was careful how he answered our questions. Since Dad was born and raised in Chico, he knew a lot of people, and could usually tell me about the deceased person. Most often he'd say he or she lived a long life and died of old age.

Dad later revealed he had been careful talking about cancer, sickness, or anything unexpected, because as a child I could have believed that if I were to get sick then I'd end up in the box. I learned a lot about old age in my childhood.

Dad worked with employees who also had young children. We kids played hide-and-go-seek at the funeral home or the cemetery. I know that may sound weird, but to us it wasn't. We didn't look at playing in the cemetery any differently than playing in the park. The deceased were kept in refrigeration and we were forbidden to play in other sensitive areas.

Dad was working at a funeral home out of town for a little while and I remember going there with my mom. It had a basement where the caskets were stored. My sister Destiny and I went down there and played around. I admit, playing in the basement was a little creepy but to us girls, the venture was just another day with Dad at work.

Not only did my sisters and I play hide-and-go-seek in the cemeteries but we also went into the prep room with Dad while he worked. Dad told me, when I got older, that I was the curious one. I wanted to come into the prep room and see what he was doing. It wasn't until I was in my teens that I really understood what Dad did in there. But as a child, it seemed like our dad was a doctor—practicing his skills on the dead.

Shawntel, ready for first hearse road-trip with Dad (casket in backseat)

Sisters Shawntel and Destiny playing at Chico Cemetery

Shawntel turns cartwheels in cemetery

Pet Funerals

MY SISTERS AND I went to Chico Christian Preschool. Some of our best memories are from there. Mom told me that when I graduated from preschool, all the kids had to get up in front of the class and tell the audience what they wanted to do when they grew up. The little kids were saying, "firefighters," "nurses," or "teachers." I got up there, took that microphone, and proclaimed, "When I grow up I want to be a *mommy*." Little did I know I was on the path of becoming a funeral director/embalmer.

Whenever our pet animals died we held small funerals for them and a burial in our backyard. I will never forget the first experience I had with death and denial at the age of six. I came home from school one day and was eager to see my cat, Simba. I was searching and searching for him ... no luck. Then Mom told me I needed to talk to Dad and ask him why I wasn't able to find Simba. Contractors, who were installing cabinets in the house, accidentally set a cabinet on top of my cat. Dad sat me down and told me Simba died. There was no "beating around the bush," Dad was straight to the fact that my cat had died. He asked if I wanted to see Simba. Of course I wanted to see him (Dad thought it would be alright for me to see/touch him since Simba looked okay). I held Simba and cried for hours. We had a burial for him. We said a short prayer for the cat and I placed him, wrapped in a blanket, into the hole Dad dug. I felt empty and angry. I don't remember this very well, but my parents told me it started raining that night and I went outside with a shovel and tried to exhume Simba. I wanted him back. Dad came out, held me closely in the rain, and said Simba was not coming back. There are many stages of grief we go through after a death. I learned some of them at a young age.

I imagine many people may disagree with how Dad handled the situation. Some parents would replace the cat with another one or tell their child the cat ran away. They wouldn't tell their child the cat died. Not for me; when there was a death, we were told. I don't think being told about a death is bad, if anything I think that it's healthy. Obviously, so did my parents. We've had other pets die and held funerals for each one.

I will never forget the first time I saw Mom and Dad both cry. We had responded to an ad for puppies and selected a golden retriever from their litter to bring home. It was Christmastime. That night my youngest sister Vanessa let the sweet puppy outside. A short while later, Mom asked where is the puppy? We flipped on the pool light and sadly discovered our puppy motionless in the swimming pool. Mom yelled for me to get Dad's help. I ran and banged on the door for him to come save the dog. Dad raced outside but it was too late. He tried to revive the puppy but was unsuccessful. The whole family cried. We buried our unnamed puppy.

Mom phoned the family that gave us the puppy, crying as she told them about the tragedy. The next day we received a surprise at our door: a new golden retriever puppy that we named Sparky.

First Kiss

AFTER CHICO CHRISTIAN Preschool, we went to public school. Since we lived so close, Destiny and I pedaled our rainbow colored bikes to John McManus Elementary (yes, rainbow colored ... they were so cool) and felt pretty grown up.

Let me give you a little background on my social skills. At Bidwell Junior High I wasn't necessarily a "cool kid," but I wasn't a total loser either. I had a few good friends in junior high. I ate in the cafeteria, however, the cool kids ate lunch outside on the benches. A classmate came into the cafeteria and invited me to go outside and eat with them. I'm sure she could tell by the look on my face that I was a little uncomfortable with the offer and totally felt like I was in a movie as the nerd stepping up on the popularity pole—which, now that I think about it—I was that nerd! I felt somewhat out of place with the kids I hardly knew, but I made friends quickly. From then on, I ate outside!

In junior high we had school dances. Since I was now a cool kid I went with my new friends and got to dance with some cute boys. Of course, as junior highers, we danced about a foot away from each other ... but we still looked pretty cool. I laugh at this now, but when my friends and I went to the dances, we asked our parents to not drop us off in front of the gym, but near the back so we weren't seen with them. Ahh the things we do as junior highers.

I met my first boyfriend, George, in junior high; a cool kid with the bluest eyes. He asked me to be his girlfriend and we held hands down the hallways. It really made me feel like a cool kid. I was really nervous when we said good-bye because I was scared he'd go in for a kiss and I would freak out. Sure enough, George kissed me for the first time and I freaked out. I had never been kissed before (well, besides when I was quite younger with my neighbor, but that doesn't count).

I told Mom George kissed me and I pretended to her I didn't like it. I had freaked, but there was a part of me that didn't mind the kiss. I see why parents dread their daughters getting older and into boys. George and I didn't last very long. He moved away, which didn't upset me. At that age I was so occupied with my social life and sports that my "love" feelings had not developed. Throughout my junior high years I made more friends, my athletic abilities improved, and I joined a swim team, which I learned to love as a sport. The next thing I knew I was in high school. I ditched the rainbow colored bike for an '89 Honda Accord.

High school was a fun time but also eye-opening. I had many great friends, my confidence was better (after surpassing the awkward stage in junior high), and I was passionately involved with sports and my education. I started dating a football player, Robert, my freshman year. He was cute, smart, and very athletic. We made a great couple. I went to his football games and was the first to greet him afterwards with a kiss. One Friday, after the game, I rushed over to greet him with a kiss and he broke up with me.

He told me he was seeing someone else. I was not only shocked, but very embarrassed. I was hurt, sad, and having flashbacks of my junior high days eating in the cafeteria. Thank goodness I got over him fast!

Soon after losing the football player, I dated a basketball player. We enjoyed many school dances together. I should have been more wary of these jocks. The basketball player lasted a couple months; things just didn't work out. After that I swore I'd never date a jock again. Right. …

AT THE BEGINNING of my sophomore year I had been single for a good while. I was really into softball and swimming, working part-time at Gottschalks in the mall to save money for a car (that's where the '89 Honda comes into play), and taking a full load of classes. A friend asked me if I'd go to lunch with her and her boyfriend. I agreed. Little did I know her boyfriend was bringing a friend, Derrick. It was like a blind date. He was a soccer player and a year older than me. I was really hesitant about him because I had sworn off jocks a while ago—they seemed to not work out for me. Derrick was different (we have all said this before). He was very good-looking and athletic … my weaknesses! Yikes. After lunch we exchanged numbers and started to hang out a bit.

I went to Derrick's soccer games and wore his jacket. I put notes in the pockets. I felt special. He asked me to be his girlfriend and of course, I said yes. Derrick was my first real boyfriend! I met his entire family, went on trips with him, and pretty much did everything with him. However (you saw this coming), I will never forget the day Derrick cheated on me. I was ready to go to my softball game but it was canceled due to rain. Everyone was excited because now we could just mess around and play with our free time. I went to see my soccer boyfriend. Derrick was acting weird; like he was in trouble. I ignored his demeanor and didn't think anything of it.

Derrick came over to my house that night. While he was there I got a phone call from a girlfriend who told me Derrick had kissed another girl at a party. I didn't want to believe it. My boyfriend was cheating on me? No way! I thought I was beyond boys who cheated. I asked Derrick about it and he confessed making a stupid mistake that will never happen again. Red flag! This was about three months into our relationship, just long enough for this to make me upset. I didn't talk to Derrick for a couple days. He was trying to make things up to me. I ended up forgiving him and we were able to move on. It took time to regain the trust, but we got it back.

Derrick and I developed a strong relationship throughout our high school years. My sisters became so close to Derrick that they called him brother. I thought I was going to marry this guy. Derrick was the first guy *ever* that I said those three words to: "I love you."

Derrick and I were telling each other "I love you." He regained his trust with me and we were on a good path—a path to what I thought could be forever.

Writing on the Walls

TOWARDS THE END of my junior year I was voted basketball princess for my class. This meant I would be joined by the other class princesses walking down a red carpet with our dads. The princesses wore crowns and my favorite part, a gown. I was honored and excited my classmates elected me. However, consequences came with this crown.

People started saying hurtful things behind my back after my name was announced as class princess. I overheard some girls saying I didn't deserve it. Other mean-spirited comments were going around and I saw writing about me on the bathroom walls. I was in the girls locker room getting ready for class and saw a girl had written on the stall "Shawntel is a stuck-up bitch." I tried to wash it off—I was embarrassed and felt really vulnerable. Girls whispered about me in the hallways which made me feel so awful I wanted to hide under a rock. I remember crying to my parents about this. They gave me the best advice, "Don't let other people define your reality." I had never thought about that. I learned very quickly not to let other people put me down. I grew tougher skin and learned paying attention to smears is not worth the heartache. I guess this was my first crude awakening with people who say hurtful things to make themselves feel better. It was hard getting used to them.

Despite the rumors, writings on the walls, and negativity, Dad and I had fun the night of the game. My mom and aunt did my hair and I put on the beautiful gown I bought. We were picked up in a limo, went to an amazing dinner with the other girls and their dads, then walked down the red carpet in front of hundreds of people. I felt so special. All the negativity I had experienced was gone the moment I started walking down the red carpet with my dad by my side and my friends and family in the audience. Derrick handed me a bouquet of roses after the game, then took me home. We watched movies till we fell asleep. Life was really good.

Dad and homecoming princess Shawntel Newton

Simpson University

THE SENIOR YEAR at Pleasant Valley High was fun but I was ready to graduate. I had a lot of wonderful friends I knew would last a lifetime. Both sisters and I were very close and looked up to each other. We did lots of things as a family—dinners, vacations, and church were a big part in our lives. No one could break us apart.

My senior year was probably my favorite. I had completed the hard classes as a junior, so my last year would be a breeze. I was team captain of the swim team. My relationship with Derrick was strong—we loved each other and talked about someday getting married. But before marriage I wanted to think about college. So many questions went through my head: Where to go? Should I leave Chico? Junior college or a university? Private or public? What do I major in? All these thoughts went through my head like most soon-to-be graduates.

Most of my closest friends planned on going to nearby Butte College, but I felt like I needed to get out of town and live on my own; I was eighteen. I started looking and applying to different colleges. My parents thought it would be a great idea if I considered attending a private university for at least one year. I thought ... *no way*. I had attended public school from K–12. There's no way I'd want to be in a private school. My dad went to Biola for one year in Southern California and my mom went to a private college for a couple years.

I decided to research private universities in California and learned very quickly private colleges are not cheap. Holy cow!! My parents always told us girls that as long as we are in school, they would help pay for our education. So with that said, I applied to Simpson University in Redding, California. I was accepted and moved into the dorms with three other girls. The bonus for me was Derrick had enrolled in Shasta College, also in Redding. This was a win-win for me.

I went into Simpson University with a slightly big head thinking this is going to be a cakewalk. I will dominate in my Bible classes. I have watched all the cartoons on Jesus, *Veggie Tales*, picture books, and I had my own Bible. Well, let's just say that I was wrong. Apparently, I didn't know the Bible as well as I thought.

I took a full load my first semester. Four of us roommates shared a small room plus one bathroom. This was a challenge! Thank goodness my friend Summer, whom I've known most of my life, was one of my roommates. Summer's boyfriend also went to Simpson. The other two were from Alaska and the East Coast. I felt like I was off to a good start.

My parents helped me move. I wasn't allowed to bring any animals, but could bring Fred, a beta fish I had for a couple years. After my parents got me settled in, I didn't want them to leave me. I started to get a little homesick even though I was only an hour away from home. I still felt sad. I had to realize I actually had it really good. Derrick

Shawntel and her dad, Ric Newton, at Simpson University, first day of college

lived in the same town, a friend lived in the dorms, oh and I had my fish, Fred. I needed to stop complaining.

Like I mentioned, once I started classes I realized I did not know the Bible as well as I thought. I felt like I was this horrible sinner among all these "goodie-good Christian" kids whose parents were all pastors. I didn't mention my parents' profession to the students—I didn't want them to get weird on me. I was really missing my family. It wasn't easy being away from my sisters, parents, and friends. Here's where things got worse ...

About a month into college, Derrick called me out of the blue and said he wanted to explore his college years *without* a girlfriend. I asked him to repeat what he just told me. I was literally in shock. I cried on the phone. I was already vulnerable and had no clue what to do next. I am not a big crier, but I think that night I bawled enough to last a lifetime. I thought I was going to marry this guy. My family loved him, I loved him, and I didn't know how I was going to go on without him.

I woke up the next day, puffy eyes and all. Summer was brushing her teeth by my bed (our beds were on each of the four corners of the room. Above our heads were shelves for books and such). "Shawntel, why is Fred not in his bowl?" Summer asked. The first thing that came to mind was ewww, Fred jumped out of his bowl and landed in my hair. I got up and searched around my pillows and bed—no Fred! Then I looked on the shelves above my bed and found Fred dead next to his bowl. Are you kidding me? Why is this happening to me? Derrick just broke up with me, I suck at the Bible, I have like no friends here, and now I have to find my pet fish dead. I locked myself in the bathroom for hours and didn't come out. Oh, and to top it off, that is where I convened little Fred's burial … in the toilet.

I called my mom to help me feel better. She told me to go to my aunt's house to get my mind off things. Mom's sister lived in Redding. I visited her and focused on other things. She made me feel better. The next day two of my best girlfriends took me to lunch. I vented to them about Derrick and of course recounted the horror of finding my only pet dead on the shelf above my head.

My parents sent emails encouraging me to be strong and things will get better. I needed to move forward. I started going through more stages of grief. It was not easy to move on from my relationship with Derrick. His emails and calls to say he misses me but needs to explore things on his own didn't help. I thought, well the only way I am going to get over our relationship is to not talk with him, email, or see him until I've healed. Let those stages of grief begin.

I CAME HOME for Christmas break. I wasn't sure if I wanted to finish another semester or not, but both parents encouraged me to finish out the year and then decide what to do next. It was nice spending Christmas break with my family, which helped with my healing of Derrick's breakup. I was thankful to have my family there for me.

After the break, I drove back to Simpson University and started crying. I wasn't enthused about attending another semester without Derrick. Then I found out Summer wasn't returning. She and her boyfriend decided to move back to Chico. I looked at the situation from a new perspective: without soccer boyfriend, Summer, or my fish, I could start focusing on schooling, making new friends and memories.

It was a rough start, though. I was still struggling in Bible class (no surprise there). I decided to tell my Bible teacher I was trying to do well in class, and I'm normally an A student. I ended up crying because I was embarrassed (obviously, crying was not foreign to me anymore). Never before had I conferred with a teacher about my grades. I was an A/B student all my life. And now I was getting a D (yes, D as in David, from the Bible … I knew that much as least). The teacher assured me as long as he saw some improvement, he'd make sure I'd pass the class. Phew, thank you, Lord. I was doing really well in all my other classes; it was just the Bible I was having a hard time with.

Now that I had my studies down, it was time to open up to my classmates and make some friends. I needed to bring out the social skills I gained from junior high school and make up for last my semester of reclusiveness.

A new roommate, Blondie, replaced Summer. Blondie and I got along very well. She was close to my age and from down south. We started to do a lot of things together. She was like me: very open and wanting to move on from the past, and she wanted to have fun in college together. She helped inspire me to improve.

I opened up further to classmates, went on road trips with friends, and attended basketball games. One day Mom visited and asked, "Wow, what happened to my shy daughter?" I just sprouted into this "Miss Talkative." This was so true. In junior high and high school I was not a very talkative person. I was actually pretty shy. Since Simpson, I had been conversing more and stepping out of my comfort box. Mom was the first to make me realize that, believe it or not, Simpson University, the school I hated, was changing me … for the good.

My psychology class inspired me. Learning about different ways of life and how we all go about our daily lives started me thinking. During class I asked myself, what am I going to do with my life? I didn't even know what my interests were or what I would be good at. One unforgettable day, while in my psychology class, we had to take the Myers-Briggs test to help us find our passion in life. I had never taken a test like it before so I was curious. There were a series of questions to answer such as do you like working with people, and do you like to sit at a desk … on and on and on. There were a least a couple hundred questions. When it finally came time for me to click the results button, I was anxious to see what the computer came up with.

Results Button

WHAT WAS MY passion in life? The Myers-Briggs test answered: *Funeral Director!* Ummm ... this is *not* real, *no way!* Funeral director—you have to be kidding me. Is God playing a joke on me? Did my dad rig this computer? I don't believe this. Funeral directors don't appear on tests like that. No one really wants to be a funeral director. Growing up, I sure did *not* want to do what Dad did. I think the entire world heard me gasp. My brain was going crazy. I started to think, there has to be a reason why this answer came up. I mean, doesn't my dad just bury bodies and that's it? What more comes with this job that, apparently, I'd be good at? Many questions went through my mind that day. I literally walked to my dorm dumbfounded.

I grew up around death, but I never considered becoming part of the funeral industry—I never imagined I'd be interested in the profession. Maybe there was more to the job than I thought. Feeling overwhelmed with confusion, I called my parents.

When Dad heard funeral director was in my category of future jobs, I think he jumped for joy. He was excited, but remained quiet about it (probably because he didn't want to scare me away). I kept the test result to myself for a while (aside from my parents) because I didn't want to believe it. It was not settling well with me. I think I was in denial with it. I went to the cafeteria for breakfast and talked to one of my professors—it was my Bible teacher who, thankfully, passed me at the end of the year. I decided to tell him about my crazy experience with the results button. I told him my dad owns a funeral home and I never wanted to be a part of the business, other than having to go there because we couldn't get a babysitter. "Well, what exactly does your dad do at his job?" he asked. I looked at him and thought, hmmm, I don't really know. I just know many people find his profession very strange and creepy. And that he places people in boxes. I really didn't know what went on within my dad's line of work. I just remember things from when I was little, and that's not a whole lot.

THAT MOMENT AT Simpson University was a turning point in my life. I wasn't sure if it was going to be for the better, or worse, which was the scary thing. I still try to ignore the fact I was just told, by a computer, I should be a funeral director and embalmer. I finished out my year at Simpson University and made my way over to Shasta College, still living in Redding.

Goodbye Simpson University and hello junior college. I decided to take general education classes and move out of the dorms. I ended up with a roommate who also switched from Simpson University. We were so excited starting Shasta College. We signed a one-year lease. I now felt like a true college student with an apartment, roommate, and lots of bills. I got a job with a pharmacy as a tech and learned very quickly that people want their medicine fast and cheap.

One story from the pharmacy I will never forget is about Mr. and Mrs. Smith. I think you'll get a laugh from it. ...

I WAS HAVING a bad day. My hours were long and I dealt with a lot of upset patients. A cute elderly couple holding hands walked up to the counter. I guessed they were in their early eighties by the way they were walking, talking, and laughing with each other. Mr. Smith introduced himself and his wife and told me they've been married for over sixty years and they both are in their nineties. I thought, whatever they are doing to stay looking this healthy, I want to make sure I do it, too. They had come to get his prescription. I went in back where we kept the files and pulled Mr. Smith's. He was in to pick up Viagra.

I was a little shocked seeing "Viagra" on a pill bottle for a ninety-year-old man. I was my professional self and didn't comment about the prescription when I rang him up. The total amount was quite a bit for just some pills, and I was waiting to hear him complain after I told him the price (a lot of customers got upset when I told them their total, so I was used to people getting angry). With Mr. and Mrs. Smith, it was another story. He was *not* upset and smiled as he paid for the pills. "We may need a little help sometimes, but we still keep that spark in our marriage." I sat there thinking about what Mr. Smith had just said to me, and I realized that he's so right—sometimes a little help is not a bad thing, and there should always be a spark! I handed them their pills. "Have a great day," I said. "We will now," Mr. Smith replied as he waved the bag of Viagra in front of me.

I will never forget the loving couple. They made my day a lot better.

WHILE WORKING AT the pharmacy and going to class in Redding, my roommate announced she was moving back home, out of state. I didn't know anyone who could replace her. Thankfully I knew whom to turn to for advice. I called Aunt Connie. I was in tears. I was worried about my options. Connie worked at a small Christian college in Redding and put notice in the bulletin that she had a niece looking for a roommate. Thankfully, I got someone to share the apartment.

I WAS TAKING a small load of classes at Shasta Junior College. I loved the interpersonal communications course. I discovered I was good with interpersonal skills. I knew this was a gift because talking in front of groups came naturally for me. I just wasn't ready to admit these skills would be beneficial for a funeral director.

Even though I didn't want to acknowledge the odds of me becoming a funeral director were pretty high, I took a death and dying class to see if I would find any interest or feelings about the subject. I walked in and saw only two students in the small classroom. Well, that answered my questions—no one wants to learn about this, talk about it, or even mention the word death (aside from two other students). Our professor talked to us and asked why we were taking the class. I, totally lying, told him it was because I needed more credits, and the other students said the same thing. He talked twenty minutes about how we are a death-denying society and we need to be more comfortable with death and dying. I agreed with him. However, I wasn't convinced that just because I, too, think we need to be more open about death, I would become a funeral director.

Class was canceled that day for the rest of the semester.

TOWARDS THE END of the year I was driving to the store with my neighbor. After we entered the onramp, the car behind us wasn't paying attention and rear-ended us before we merged. This was not just a little bumper tap. We were slammed so hard that our car was knocked many feet ahead, almost into the oncoming traffic. My neighbor was shaking and crying, I was in shock and immobile. The car was smoking and all I thought was God please don't let the car blow up. We were stuck in the car. It seemed like a lifetime before the ambulance came.

By the time the ambulance arrived I was so scared I threw up. The paramedics took us away. I called my aunt and uncle from the ambulance to meet us at the hospital. I was still scared and prayed. Thank God Aunt Connie was nearby. Next, I called my parents at work—I needed them to be with me. I told Dad I had thrown up. He, having been at the scene of many accident calls, couldn't help but think something was really wrong; internal bleeding perhaps. Both parents were praying their entire way to Redding.

They arrived at the hospital as I was being x-rayed. I felt lonely in the small room. All I wanted was my mom. We were all praying my neighbor and I would be okay. Waiting for results was the worst part of my anxiety. The doctor came out and said I will have minor back problems, but there was no internal bleeding. Thank God.

That accident shook me up pretty good. By that time my year lease was nearly over, I was ready to move back to Chico and put myself back together—literally.

Exploring

I MOVED BACK to Chico, still not sure if funeral directing was the answer to my future. I ended up going to the local Butte College for a year to figure things out. I was single, I was with my friends again, and I was happy.

I needed a job quickly. My parents agreed to help us girls during school, but we had to contribute a lot toward expenses too. I started working at various retail stores while going to school, but I was always on the edge. I wasn't satisfied. Retail was not my thing. I got bored. I was really good with my customer service, but I wanted more of a challenge.

I lived at home again. Dad asked if I wanted to work for the funeral home. I thought, *no way.* I grew up in the funeral home—that's the last thing I wanted to do. But I couldn't help but feel this pull towards it—let alone my results on the Myers-Brigg's test. I figured I should let go of my denial and learn what working in a funeral home was all about.

BRIEF HISTORY ON my dad's funeral home: Dad worked at a funeral home in Chico as manager and went out on his own. He and his business partner Bob bought

Chico Funeral Home in 1991 and renamed it Newton–Bracewell Chico Funeral Home. They also own a mausoleum/columbarium and crematory. They have a storefront office in Paradise (which is about twenty min-

First anniversary newspaper advertisement

utes up the ridge). Their partnership is now Newton-Bracewell Inc.—an exciting business move for our entire family. They started out serving eighty families a year, and today serve over five hundred families. The growth rate shows how well they have prospered in twenty years.

Everything I had denied being interested in, thought about trying, and was advised to pursue, added up. Sure enough, the next thing I knew I was answering phones: "Newton-Bracewell Funeral Home, this is Shawntel, how may I help you?" I filed papers, answered the door, ran errands, and dusted. Not a fun job. I thought if I am going to work here, there has to be more to do than file papers.

I also learned very quickly that I was not a handywoman. I was never into tools growing up, and I definitely didn't know all the different names of these "man-tools."

The staff will never forget one incident …

I was helping an employee hang a curtain rod and he asked me to get a Philips screwdriver from the garage. I knew what a screwdriver looked like, but I didn't know there were different kinds of screwdrivers, or even different sizes. All I found in the drawer were screwdrivers that said "Stanley" on them. I continued searching through the drawer for a Philips screwdriver but was having no luck. I went back and told the employee we didn't have any Philips screwdrivers, only Stanleys. The entire staff started laughing. I was confused. I was thinking to myself, "What the heck is everyone laughing at? ... what did I say? ... is there something in my teeth?" Dad told everyone, "Well, I feel like I'm to be the one to blame for this because apparently I never taught my children anything about tools." Still, I was confused until someone explained Stanley is a brand and Philips is the actual kind of screwdriver. I felt a little silly after that. The staff still talks about the Stanley screwdriver. I guess you can say ... I had a blond moment!

Despite all the blond moments I had working for my dad, repetitively filing papers, and answering phones, I knew there had to be more to this job. There's no way Dad filed papers all day for thirty years. Dad could tell I was restless and needed more to do, so he asked if I wanted to go on a removal with him. I thought anything is better than this. When I say the word "removal," or "transfer," it means going on a death call. This could be at someone's home, hospital, accident scene, or a care home. I was actually very nervous my first removal even though I had seen death, and I have been around death all my life. There was something different this time. I was going to someone's home and I would be talking with the family.

I will never forget walking into the family's home with Dad and my heart beating fast. I was prepared for the call because he knew the deceased woman and told me about her on the way over. She was elderly and on hospice care. This wasn't going to be like a homicide or suicide call. As we walked in, Dad greeted the family and started talking with them. Not only did they feel comforted because they knew him, but because my dad took the time to meet them where they were. After talking with them for a while about the deceased woman, Dad explained he and I would bring in the gurney and gently place her on it. We brought in the gurney and the family decided to help with the removal. We all placed her on the gurney while the family said good-bye one more time. She had been sick for months, and her thin body was worn out. This experience brought to mind the story of Dad answering my childhood question, "Why are they in the box?"

While observing Dad talking with the family, I thought he was like a counselor or even a therapist. This is one of the most difficult times during someone's life, and Dad is there for the families helping them. I thought about my own interpersonal skills and how they could be used.

We took her into the funeral home. Dad said she was to be embalmed. I knew a little bit about embalming—it is a science—but only from what I remembered when I was little. Being interested about what happens next, I asked if I could shadow him. He allowed me to help, and my curiosity about this industry grew instantly. I was now thinking, hmmmm we are mixing therapy and science—all in one job. Interesting.

Funeral Arranger

I CONSULTED MY family about participating in an arrangement. I didn't know anything about meeting with grieving families. I was only twenty years old. What do I know?

My first arrangement was for a family whose grandmother died from heart disease. The arrangements had been preplanned. I watched Dad arrange the funeral and observed what he did to help the family. Preplanning means the arrangements have already been signed and paid for by the deceased. This makes things sometimes easier on the survivors, not only financially, but knowing the decisions are what the deceased wanted.

I had no idea what went into all this. I felt like my dad was a florist, caterer, counselor, mediator, and so much more. There was a lot he was doing for the family. And he only had a couple days to do it.

I decided it was time to get my feet wet. I took a state law review test and became a funeral arranger. While I took the state law review, I was completely blown away by all the rules and regulations that come with the funeral profession. This job was going to be harder than I thought.

I was really nervous going into my first arrangement by

myself. I couldn't have asked for a better family to meet with for the first time. The arrangements had already been paid for and the daughter had been expecting the death of her mother for some time.

I ordered the casket, flowers, food, tables, obituary, called the cemetery, got in touch with the pastor, music, sound, and limo drivers. I felt like I was a wedding planner, but I only had a couple days to do everything. I worked the funeral. At the end of every funeral, Dad told me, we as funeral directors go down and thank the pastor and announce the conclusion of the funeral service. I was *very* nervous. I went in front of the people and made my announcements.

Not all my arrangements were easy. In fact, as a funeral arranger, I knew things were going to get harder—not everyone dies from old age. My first difficult arrangement was for a family whose brother committed suicide. I was only twenty years old and about to step into a room of six adult siblings who did not want to be there and were very angry. What does one say in a situation like this? What words of comfort could I bring them? How could I make this better? My answer was ... there is nothing to say or do that will make this better. This was an unexpected death and they did not like having to be at the funeral home. I was the bad guy who told them where their brother was found, how he killed himself, why they couldn't view him right away, and what the expenses were going to be. This was an uncomfortable arrangement for all of us. I was sure they didn't like it that I was so young.

After the arrangements were completed I had to step outside for a moment and take in everything that just happened. This was a very serious job. I had *no* clue arrangements like these take place. I gained more respect for my dad that day.

I began meeting with families almost every day and started to help work funerals as well. We were kept very busy averaging three to four funeral services a week.

ONE OF THE first military services I worked in Chico was also the first time I drove a hearse to the cemetery. I piloted the wheel of a large boat-like limo with mixed feelings navigating between drivers and pedestrians delivering my precious cargo. I stopped, got out, stepped to the side with Dad, then shadowed him. A group of four military representatives at the cemetery folded and presented the American flag. About a hundred guests attended. Handsome gentlemen in uniform lined up shoulder to shoulder with their rifles alongside. Unexpectedly, the men fired their rifles like an explosion! I ducked for cover. I didn't know they actually go off. I thought we were being shot down. I made quite the scene. People asked if I was okay but I acted like nothing happened. I thought, if I start talking I will most likely cry from embarrassment. Dad quietly laughed at me.

That day I not only learned when there are military honors rifles will be loud and never wear heels in a cemetery—wedges work much better.

AFTER I STARTED feeling comfortable meeting with families, I wanted to continue stepping further—get into the prep room and go on more removals. I was put on our rotation with transfers, meaning that after work hours I would be on call for the funeral home so when there was a death, I would go to the home, hospital, or care home to transfer the individual to our funeral home. This took some getting used to. I was on call for the funeral home a couple times a week. This meant no making plans with friends; no dinner reservations ... basically being next to my phone at all times. It was really hard because I was working at the funeral home as a funeral arranger, going to school part-time, and being on call a couple times a week.

I would get calls really late at night. Sometimes I got called out three times, then had to be at work the next day ready to go. It was not easy. Respect continued to grow for my dad and all the sacrifices he made for us.

I had trouble going back to sleep after getting a call in the middle of the night. I developed more empathy for my dad who was on call pretty much 24/7 when I was little. And I was complaining about being on call two times out of the week? This routine reminded me when my sisters and I would hear the garage door open knowing Dad was finally home. That's exactly what I was doing now.

Being on call didn't always mean going on a removal. Sometimes callers wanted to talk about arrangements or prices. One time a gentleman had just found his significant other dead in the apartment. He called the police but they had not arrived. Before I could calm him down or try to get some information, he told me he was contemplating killing himself. I was thinking, what the heck am I getting myself into? I am not a suicide helpline, I don't know what to say. My heart started racing. I could tell he was not sober—he wasn't making a lot of sense. He told me he did not have a gun but felt he couldn't go on living anymore without his loved one. I told him not to do anything until helped reached him. He asked me to stay on the phone with him and I said yes. The police arrived, got on his phone, and said they would call back when they were ready for us. I hung up and felt like I had been hit by a bus. I was in my early twenties and had been talking to a man who wanted to kill himself. I could not believe how difficult things can be at times—even a phone conversation. My job kept getting more complex.

Since Chico is a small town, we don't see a lot of homicides or suicides, but when they happen, my dad would frequently be one of the first to know. When I was very young he told me a tragic story about a little boy and girl who were murdered. He and his business partner went on the call but weren't warned of the horrible situation. Dad told me he walked into the house of dead children and instantly thought about us girls at home. He had nightmares for many nights and said that call will follow him forever. Hearing a story like that from Dad made me wonder … can I handle something like that? I felt too young to be getting into situations like his. However, I knew I had a gift and I needed to explore things more.

MY FIRST UNEXPECTED death job was removing a man who drank himself to death five days earlier in his home. He had hepatitis and was emitting a *very* strong odor. I was in my skirt and heels but changed to a pair of flat shoes kept in the van for cases such as this. I had never seen death look this bad. He was unrecognizable.

Another funeral director and I put on protective clothing and began putting him in a body bag. Deputies were available to help us, but normally funeral directors make the removals. Surprisingly I was not bothered by the smell and was able to handle this difficult situation. The deputies took photos while we rolled his body for them to start an investigation. The pathologist arrived, took some blood samples and his temperature.

I felt like I was a part of the TV show *C.S.I.* After we transferred him to the funeral home, I thought now what? Who determines the cause of death, and how? I will add, growing up I watched *C.S.I.* all the time with Mom (I think she's seen every episode). I was always into the science part of the show and not so much the drama. I tuned in more closely whenever the pathologist took samples, performed the autopsy, and talked about the cause of death. The funny thing was, I envisioned myself doing that. I really thought if I wanted to do something like that … *I could.*

Unlike most big cities that have a central morgue and an ambulance makes the transfer to the morgue where investigations and autopsies are performed, in Chico the funeral home sends someone to the place of death and is involved with the coroners and sheriff. The funeral home's prep room becomes the central morgue where the autopsies are done. I did not know the process of an autopsy, but I was curious.

When the pathologist does an autopsy, he or she needs an assistant—the funeral directors are in charge of helping. Since I was curious and already felt like I have been a part of *C.S.I.*, I thought, why not? I have already been on some interesting removals; why not assist in autopsies as well?

I jumped right in. How interesting—I have never seen an autopsy aside from television. I had no experience in this area of the prep room. Although I wasn't a licensed embalmer yet, the pathologist agreed to let me assist him. This I will ever forget.

I was nervous. I was gowned from head to toe in protective equipment. Thank goodness the pathologist was in a good mood with me because I was talking a mile-a-minute, I was so intrigued by the procedure. I was firing off questions and seeing things I had never seen before. I felt like a little kid asking her dad question after question. The pathologist patiently responded to my enthusiasm.

I experienced death at a young age, but not autopsies. I took his notes, weighed organs, held instruments for him, and tried to help as much as I could. The doctor not only made an incision on the abdomen to take samples of the organs, he also performed a cranial autopsy. I've taken an anatomy class but this was different ... so different!

After the autopsy, it's the assistant's job to suture the incisions and to make sure everything is replaced with the body. I sutured the incisions and thought, I want to be a pathologist!

I enjoyed assisting and asked what's involved to become a pathologist. Well, let's just say once I heard how many years of schooling are required, I said, *forget that*. I will be just fine assisting. It would take about ten years to get into the profession, and I didn't even want to think about all the loans I would have to take out. I moved on from that idea very quickly.

Assisting autopsies raised my interest in the science of embalming. I watched Dad embalm when I was younger, and I walked into the prep room as a funeral arranger every now-and-then out of curiosity. I had not actually watched an embalming from beginning to end. My curiosity, once again, got the best of me and I looked into being an embalmer.

Pathologist to Embalmer

I WAS STILL a funeral arranger, I was going on removals in the middle of the night, I was meeting with families, and assisting in autopsies. Yet, there was still more I wanted to be involved with. Embalming has been in practice for centuries. The Egyptians had a unique way of embalming. Since then, we have turned embalming into a great science. I did not know a lot about the science of embalming, but after assisting in an autopsy and seeing the anatomy first hand, I wanted to learn the art of preserving bodies.

In order to become an embalmer within California I would need to attend mortuary school and take a state test. I had doubts I was ready to enroll in mortuary school. I wanted to make sure I even liked this work. I decided to become an apprentice first. To become an apprentice I had to fill out state paperwork, be willing to work full-time in the funeral home, and assist in twenty-five embalmings with a licensed embalmer. After the first twenty-five, I would embalm unassisted as an apprentice a total of one hundred embalmings within two years. Following apprenticeship, enrollment in mortuary school is required to become fully licensed.

I didn't want to get my dad's hopes up too high, but decided it wouldn't hurt to start my apprenticeship and see where it leads. Yes, the "results button" was still haunting me. But so far, I have been completely intrigued by the profession.

I will never forget entering the prep room to assist Dad in my first embalming. I felt pretty confident—if I can assist a pathologist with an autopsy I can assist my dad with an embalming. How hard can it be? Before Dad came into the prep room, I thought I could start by taking out instruments for him and setting out some of the chemicals I have seen embalmers use. There were *so* many different instruments I had no idea which ones he needed; nor did I know what any of them were used for; I just thought he needed one of each. The instruments all looked like something a doctor would use during surgery—I was more intrigued.

Everything I thought he needed was laid out for him. I was ready. Dad came in and said he wouldn't need all those instruments. He appreciated my initiative. Then he used a couple of the chemicals I placed out for him, but he also took out a couple more (I only pulled out chemicals that had a pretty color to them). I was thinking, geeezz Dad, you are like a chemist, restorative artist, and a doctor. How do you know how much chemical to use? Will I blow myself up if I mix the wrong ones? I had *no* clue as these thoughts ran through my head.

I didn't know what the chemicals were used for aside from helping the embalming process. They all had weird names and index numbers on them. I was never good at chemistry in high school so I didn't know what anything meant. I just did what Dad told me, and tried to be very careful. He asked me to pour the chemicals into the embalming machine. I felt like a chemist and a doctor. I started pouring chemicals into the machine when, suddenly, chemicals spurt all over the place. ... I hadn't removed the lid of the machine. Whoops!

My confidence level just dropped. I realized I had no idea what I was doing. Dad laughed and said it was okay, this was my first time—try to relax. I cleaned up my mess, took off the lid, and was even more nervous. After I stopped shaking, he started to raise the appropriate veins and arteries. I studied every move he was making and said, "Dad, you are a doctor on the dead." How did you know how to raise those vessels, what were the names of the vessels, how do you know how much chemical to put in, what if they start swelling?

There was so much I wanted to know. Embalming was just as interesting as the autopsies. Dad recalled when he went to mortuary school he learned all about the human body and how things work. I didn't tell him at the time, but after that day in the prep room with him, I made the decision to go to mortuary school. I wanted to learn more about the embalming process and be a postmortem vascular surgeon like my dad.

We worked together for a couple hours. I think I asked questions the entire time. Thank goodness my dad has patience, just like the pathologist.

The Marine

Now THAT I have embarrassed myself enough about my first experiences in the funeral industry, I will segue into a relationship I went through to get to where I am today.

During most of my apprenticeship training I was not in a relationship. I was living at home contemplating my Myers-Briggs results button. I had been on a couple dates here and there, but for the most part I remained single to focus on my career ... or at least I tried to. Then there was the marine, Lane. I was almost twenty-one when I met this man covered in tattoos with a shaved head. He was a year older than I and he, too, grew up in Chico. I was usually not attracted to guys with a lot of tattoos and known as bad kids. I was warned by many friends he was not that great of a guy and he would probably hurt me.

Naively, I started dating him. He was in the marines on leave. I found that very attractive, along with his tattoos and bad boy attitude. His mother got sick and died shortly after we started dating. After her death, he was honorably discharged and moved back to Chico. I became his care-giver, badly wanting to help him. Months went by and I began falling in love. I had been in love only once before, with Derrick.

Lane held back a lot with my family. He felt uncomfortable with our closeness. He didn't have the same experience growing up. It was hard for him to accept us even though my family tried to pull him closer. He came from a broken family. I think it was difficult for him to see me with my family.

After a year of dating and declaring how much we loved each other, I found out he was cheating on me. I, of course, did not want to believe this. I ignored it for a while. I started to resent my friends because I was mad they didn't believe he wasn't cheating. Weeks into my disbelief a friend told me she knew for a fact I was being cheated on. I confronted Lane about it and, like most guys, he denied anything ever happened. I wanted out of this misery so I called from work the girl he was supposedly seeing. I asked if rumors Lane was cheating on me were true. The hard part of talking to her was she was someone I knew and had hung out with before. She knew Lane and I were dating.

I dropped the phone when she said yes, and broke into tears feeling hurt and betrayed. Dad came out from his office. I told him what happened. Then Mom joined us and I cried some more. Once I regained my composure, I called Lane to end things with him. I always told myself never again would I be with someone who cheated on me. Lane tried to deny it, but after I told him I'd already talked to the girl, he confessed. I was devastated.

He called that night and said he was ashamed of himself. He wanted me back and promised never to hurt me again. Being the caregiver I am, his promise was really hard for me to hear. All I wanted to do was pretend his cheating never happened, move on, and be with him. I was still living with my parents and they could hear me crying myself to sleep almost nightly.

Weeks and then months went by. Lane called me off and on to apologize and make up for his cheating and lying. He told me he "found God." I was born and raised in a Christian home and always knew whomever I married would have the same faith as mine. He told me he was going to make his life better, stop drinking, and treat me the way I should be treated. He was talking with a counselor. He left flowers on my car and wrote love letters asking for forgiveness over and over. I told him I forgave him but it would take time to regain his trust. My family knew how badly I missed him. I was sucked back into the relationship with the marine.

Back together with Lane, I finally realized I needed to enroll in mortuary school. I was working in a funeral home; I might as well become fully licensed. There were only two mortuary schools in California; which makes sense because there really is not a high demand for funeral directors. One school was in the Los Angeles area, the other in Sacramento. Dad went to mortuary school in San Francisco years ago, but it closed and moved to Sacramento. I decided Sacramento, ninety miles south of Chico, would be easier to move to and I could commute my last semester if needed. I enrolled in American River College.

My family fully supported my decision to further my profession. I was looking forward to moving out of their house and getting back into an apartment; having my own independent bills again (it seems really weird I just admitted I wanted my "adult" bills again ... hmm). Lane's dad and stepmom lived in Sacramento near my apartment. How convenient. I packed and was off for a couple years feeling pretty good about starting—after all, I grew up in the business and was already an apprentice—how hard can the mortuary program be? The marine followed me to Sacramento.

I MOVED IN with another mortuary student, Jessica, who was a year ahead of me in the program. She and I got along great. We both had cats (I moved on from Fred the fish to Peaches the cat) and we enjoyed the same things (no, not just the funeral profession). I was looking forward to making new friends and starting school. It made things easier having a roommate with the same goal.

Qualifying wasn't difficult. I had to take an online class and general education, then after one semester I would officially be in the program. As far as Lane and me, we did everything together; he would even drop me off at class and pick me up. I was comfortable in our relationship, too comfortable.

Lane and I took great trip to New Orleans after the hurricane Katrina. We stayed at an old school with other churchgoers for a week to help the victims. It was humid and hot but once I was able to become selfless I realized all the devastation caused by the hurricane. We painted homes, fed the hungry, talked with families, built houses (I did the painting; not the boards and nails part), and went through the French Quarter for dinner our last night.

My caregiving skills came into play in New Orleans. I wanted to stay and help the families. The stories I heard were just awful and so tragic. The cemeteries flooded and most of the headstones were damaged. I talked with locals whose loved ones died in the hurricane. I saw homes where the waterline from flooding was apparent. Going to New Orleans made me more thankful.

After our New Orleans trip, Lane started to become obsessive. He did not like it when I talked to my friends back home. He thought they were a bad influence. Nor did he like me even talking to my parents. He didn't like me to exercise because he worried I was trying to "impress" some other guy. He wanted me all to himself, and I was blind to it all. So blind in fact, I didn't realize I wasn't talking to my best friends and family. Instead, I was only spending time with Lane. I was blinded in the relationship. I didn't notice at the time, but my caregiving was taking over my relationship and causing me to drown.

For about a year while in Sacramento I did not have the best of relationships with my family or friends. I was trapped in one with Lane that I couldn't escape. I was blind to our relationship, but deep inside of me I knew it was not healthy. I wasn't focusing on my schooling; instead, I was devoting energy to my strained relationship, trying to be the stronghold and make things work. One day, after two and a-half years of devoting my life to him, Lane woke up, took me to a homeless shelter, and had me watch him give all his belongings away. He threw his phone away—he didn't need anything materialistic. I knew Lane tended to get restless, but I never saw this coming.

Lane came to my apartment, said he was leaving for a couple years, and wait for him! He wouldn't tell me where he was going, how he was getting there, or why he was leaving. He hugged and kissed me goodbye and said he would call sometime. I was in complete shock when he left. I did not understand what just happened. Why is it these things happen to me? Why couldn't I have a healthy relationship?

I went into the closet and cried for hours. I had taken him back after he cheated on me, I lost friendships over him, and now he's just going to walk out like it's no big deal?

However, it was a blessing in disguise. I was trying too hard to rescue him and build him up throughout our relationship. It took him breaking up with me, because I couldn't do it to him, to end something that should have ended years ago. Not only had I become too comfortable, but I had this guilt inside of me that I needed to take care of him. I had been ignoring many red flags and was fighting for the relationship to work. I was the giver in the relationship, he was a taker, and I was being sucked dry. Lane wanted me all to himself on a little island where no one could interfere with us. Well, needless to say, the day the marine walked out on me was the day my life changed for good.

Back on Track

ONCE LANE LEFT me, it took a good while to grieve the loss and get back on my feet. I went through similar stages people experience with the death of a loved one. This was like a death to me. I told my family what happened. I knew they were relieved. They watched me go through a difficult relationship.

With the marine gone, God knows where, I was able to focus on my own life and get back on track. I was in mortuary school but wasn't putting my heart into it. I had been caught up in an unhealthy relationship the first semester. My relationship door closed on me, but windows were opening.

After my first semester of general education, I was accepted into the mortuary program and entered it feeling pretty good. Both of my main professors knew Dad well. He was on the board of directors for the program, and I had an advantage from growing up in the industry. Wrong! I soon learned walking into *anything* with a big head will usually bite you on the butt (or cause you to spill all over).

The program had twenty students—fifteen were women. I was surprised because I always heard the funeral industry was forever a male-dominant profession. Also, an average of forty students enroll in a mortuary program, and about twelve graduate. I just hoped I'd be one of the twelve.

The first day we were asked to do an "in class removal." I volunteered to go first. I have been on many removals and this would be a piece of cake. My roommate Jessica volunteered with me. We went to the front of the room, each got on one side of the gurney, then, as we began lowering it to the floor, *my jeans split down the front!* The entire class heard the tear. Mind you, the ripping sound was so loud it was like a movie of an over-exaggerated piece of paper tearing. But in this case, it was my jeans! I looked down and saw my pants had completely torn. Everyone saw it.

I stood up completely embarrassed and announced, "Ummm I am sure you all know, but I totally just ripped my pants." It helped sooth my embarrassment to simply acknowledge it and laugh at myself. My professor was embarrassed for me; he didn't know what to say. He gave me a sheet to wrap around my waist. The class clapped for me when I sat down. Then all the girls went into the back room to make sure their pants weren't going to tear when it was their turn. I think I broke the ice for our class, as well as becoming humble on the first day. I tend to learn the hard way!

During the first year of mortuary school I studied hard. They were not easy courses. I was taking: anatomy, chemistry, microbiology, pathology, physiology, religion, and counseling classes. I had never been so challenged in my life. The year was focused on studying, studying, and more studying. I drank a lot of coffee and lacked a social life outside of the program. Many students were confused why we had to take so many science classes like a nurse would. I was one of those students. I asked the professor why pathology or chemistry was a required course (I think we were all bitter because they were hard classes)? They're necessary, he explained, because an embalmer needs to know what happens to a body after death. There is a lot of chemistry involved and we had to learn which ones are needed for someone who died from kidney failure, was very endemic, or emaciated. Once we were told those scenarios, I realized I better start studying more!

In one class I didn't really have to study, but I had to get my hands dirty. I took restorative art for a semester. Its purpose was to teach us how to restore faces. Former students told me this was not going to be an easy class and be prepared for frustration. Great! The first day of class our professor told us to select someone's face we wanted to replicate. It could be a celebrity, friend, sister, brother, or anyone whose profile you had a picture of. We could only use photos to make their face. We had to buy a plastic face skull and a large bag of wax. During the semester many students asked why were we required to do this? "Because, there will be a time in your career you will have to restore a deceased face," the instructor explained. "They may be in a car accident, homicide, or something else causing part of their face to be destroyed and you will know the technique to restore their appearance."

I once asked Dad if he ever had to restore an accident victim's face. He told me about a meeting with a family whose son died in a motorcycle accident and his entire left side was tragically affected. The family wanted an open casket for the son's friends and family to see him one last time. Knowing the condition of the man's body, Dad told the family if he could get a couple photos of their son's face he would try and do what he could to make their son look good. The family knew his face had been affected. Dad wanted to prepare them in case he couldn't satisfy their request. After meeting with the family he went into the prep room, embalmed the man, and worked for hours while remembering the techniques he learned from mortuary school. He restored the left side of the man's face and the grateful family was able to have an open casket viewing for their son.

Throughout the class we learned each part of the face little by little—all the measurements, angles, and distances. I decided to use my youngest sister for this project and took many photos of her profile. She did not like the idea of me using her as a "deceased face." However, one of the benefits of being the oldest: younger siblings usually listen to you. So she went along with it.

We all worked hard making our faces and learning how to sculpt an ear, nose, closed eyes, wrinkles, necks, and lips. Funeral directors have to restore noses and ears the most (of course those are the hardest to mold). After weeks of finally finishing my sister's replica, I learned how to match makeup to different skin tones. I figured I'd be good at that since I'm a girl and I apply makeup every day. I should know all about matching makeup to skin tones. Little did I know, makeup is a lot different on wax and the makeup used on the deceased's skin is a lot different than the makeup I use at home. I matched the makeup well to my little sister's skin tone. I bought a blond wig as the last step.

The face was done! I received an A on my project and brought it to my parents' house for Vanessa to see. She about freaked out. "Oh my gosh, is that what I look like?... ewwww!" I told her I earned a good grade based on the photos I used. She did not care about my grade, she cared

Facial restoration project is completed

about how her "face" looked. We all had a good laugh and she put her face up in the closet so no one could see it.

After I became a pro at molding faces, ripping my pants, and drinking lots of coffee, I managed to get through a good year of mortuary school and make great friends in the program. I even became vice president of our club. I decided it was a good time to move back to Chico and commute my last two semesters so I could work while I went to school. This wasn't long after the marine had left me. The timing was good. I borrowed my sister's truck, packed everything I owned in one load, and headed north. I donated a lot of things to the Salvation Army because they reminded me of the marine and I didn't want his memory anymore. I was starting a new chapter in my life, and it felt wonderful to come home.

Returning to Chico was the best decision I made for myself. I was in my parents' house *again* and back to work. I was very happy knowing I was only two semesters away from graduating and becoming a licensed funeral director and embalmer. My classes continued to get harder and harder; I put all my energy into them. It was draining at times to be working at the funeral home, meeting with families, embalming, and commuting a couple times a week. There were times I would come into work directly from school, ninety minutes away.

One time on my way to work from Sacramento, I received a phone call from one of my best friends. She was crying. A classmate from high school, Katy, just committed suicide. We all grew up playing sports together but lost touch during college. I told my friend I would call the funeral home to make sure we were going to be taking care of the family and I could meet with the family the next day. When I called the funeral home, Mom said Katy's parents wanted to meet with me that evening to go over arrangements.

This was the first time I met with a family of someone I knew. I did not know how I was going to handle everything. I came into the funeral home actually feeling nervous about seeing Katy's body. Two of our funeral directors had gone to Katy's house to transfer her to the funeral home.

I have seen deceased bodies all my life, but I had never felt this personal emotion before. I had to view her because her family did not want to see her and I needed to check if she had jewelry on to give the family.

I asked my dad to accompany me into the refrigeration to view her. I never asked him to go in there with me before and it was a weird feeling. Dad was with me, which helped. Katy was lying on a table. I didn't know what to say. She was wearing a cross necklace which I removed for the family.

The family met me and I cried with them as they told me how much they were going to miss their daughter. Katy had been going through a rough time and dropped out of school, they said. They wanted her to be cremated and have a memorial service at our funeral home. We made the arrangements and set up a time for that weekend. I gave them the necklace. Her mom looked at me and said she had given it to Katy for her birthday.

I learned my grief was taking a toll throughout the week of meeting with the family. I became very protective of the arrangements, wanted to be the one who cremated Katy, and made sure everything was done under my care. A lot of times during a normal workday we, as funeral directors, help each other—some will meet with a family, while someone else can be in the prep room, or in the crematory area. However, this time, I wanted to do it all—Katy was my friend. I did not want anyone else to help. Now that I look back on this, I realize this was my way of grieving.

We held Katy's memorial service that weekend. We had open sharing. I had things I wanted to share and am glad I did. I talked about growing up with her and playing sports together. I made myself laugh and cry during my sharing. I saw a lot of my friends from high school whom I hadn't seen in many years. I was thankful to see everyone, and to be a part of my friend's memorial. I would not have wanted it any other way!

I WAS BLESSED to have a family business that helped me financially during school and allowed me study time when needed. My mortuary program was offering a scholarship to three students and my professor suggested I apply. I didn't think I'd be selected because I knew a lot of struggling students deserved the scholarship more than I.

I wrote my application paper then waited to hear back. The requirement of the paper was to tell the board of di-

Baby Shawntel wearing CFDA sweatsuit. Years later, the organization awarded her a scholarship.

rectors how and why I am in the mortuary school and what could I bring to the program to better it. I received a phone call saying I was one of the finalists selected to be interviewed for the scholarship. I drove down to Sacramento and met with five members of the California Funeral Directors Association (CFDA). The encouraging thing was, my dad was past president of CFDA when I was younger, so the five members knew Dad. I thought, either this could be a good thing ... or a bad thing. I better make a good impression.

The interview went well. They asked how I got into the profession, why I wanted to be a funeral director and embalmer, what my goals were, and how well am I doing in school? I think they enjoyed my answers ... especially "how I got into the profession."

A couple weeks later I received an email—I was chosen as one of the three scholarship recipients. I was going to receive five hundred dollars and the Robert Smith Award in San Jose during the CFDA presidents' banquet. I was so thankful.

CFDA paid my travel expense to San Jose. Both of my parents came to watch me receive the award.

When we arrived at the San Jose convention, I felt comfortable with everyone and was happy to be there. I met funeral directors from all over California and wasn't surprised they knew my parents and had nothing but great things to say about our funeral home. My parents were proud of me and I was grateful.

During the banquet I was so nervous about the award I didn't get to enjoy the food. My parents were asked to come on stage after I had been given a lengthy introduction. They were told CFDA was excited to present their award to me. I cried as I was called to the stage. It was overwhelming to see my parents standing with me. It meant so much. I was honored by the award and scholarship.

We celebrated that night, and I ate *a lot*. I was relaxed!

Hospital

I CONTINUED COMMUTING to American River College a couple times a week—scholarship in hand. It was time for our class to gain experience at the Sacramento County morgue under the scope of our professor.

During the last semester of the mortuary program we had to complete ten embalmings. One of those embalmings had to be accompanied by our professor with six other students. I wanted to complete the requirement and was one of the first volunteers to get my "hands dirty." Since I lived in Chico, it would be easier to stay in Sacramento with one of my classmates, Trish, and drive together early in the morning to the morgue. The next week I met up with her. This was my first visit to her apartment, which was on the side of town unfamiliar to me.

We were both exhausted from school and work. We decided to go out for dinner then go to bed early. Throughout the evening Trish was complaining of her stomach hurting and sharp pains in her lower abdomen. We both thought it was just cramps and didn't think much about it though she started being unable to walk without hunching over. Trish began to cry. I didn't know what to do, other than suggest we get her to the emergency room in case this was serious.

I drove Trish to the hospital around 7:00 P.M. There was a long waiting time for the emergency room. Finally, we met the nurses who began taking tests. They said she would have to wait for the doctor before they could do anything else. Trish was crying and scared, while I was also scared and confused about what was going on. Time went by until we talked to a doctor who said her white blood cells were at an abnormally high count; meaning her body was trying to fight something off. It was now midnight and we were both exhausted. Trish's pain increased. I tried comforting her to keep her mind off the pain. Knowing how many sick people I was exposed to during our five-hour wait, I was feeling nauseous.

The doctor handed Trish a liquid dye to drink. They were going to examine the coloring of her inflammation, which appeared to be with her appendix. The exam revealed she had appendicitis! They needed to retain her for surgery. Trish started crying again—she wanted to call her family for support.

It was now 2:00 in the morning. I was burned out. We were supposed to be at the county morgue in four hours. Obviously, Trish wasn't going to make it.

They took Trish in for surgery. I left the hospital not knowing what to do. I called my parents nearly in tears from being tired, scared, and upset. I had *no* idea where the county morgue was and my brain was fried. Oh, and not to mention I had no idea how to get back to Trish's apartment. I called her roommate and found my way to the apartment with her directions. I sat down but could not get to sleep. I stayed up and got a map to the morgue.

At the morgue, five other students joined me. They asked if I was okay because I looked how I felt. I told them

I was fine: *lie*. The professor met us and we went into the locker rooms to put on our professional protective equipment. Since I already had experience with embalming, I wasn't too nervous. I knew the case was most likely going to be a decomposed body with a strong odor. I have been on many removals—I could handle the smell. I was more concerned of passing out from sleep deprivation.

The embalming took the six of us five hours to complete. Most of the others were experiencing the process for the first time, so it took longer than normal. Once we were through, I went over to another classmate's apartment to sleep before class.

The long day was over at last. I was driving back to Chico and my own bed. Sure enough, I stopped halfway home for some food and the car wouldn't start. I could not believe it. I was so upset ... I started crying. From being in the hospital for eight hours and no sleep, to an embalming for another five hours, then class ... now my car died (no pun intended). Arrgggg! I waited an hour in the car for AAA to arrive and replace the battery. Okay, finally I was home in bed. I had the deepest sleep of my life.

THE SEMESTER STARTED to unwind. I was twenty-three, living with my parents, and I wanted to move out. I lived on my own on and off since I was eighteen. I was ready to be back "on" again.

I visited a friend's house where a bunch of us were hanging out having a great time in Chico. There was an unfamiliar face in the group. Most of the others knew her. I introduced myself to Elisabeth and we instantly became friends. We stayed together into the night talking and getting to know each other. She was from Humboldt, California, moved to Chico to attend school, and was living on her own. She didn't have a boyfriend. I told her I was living with my parents and ready to move out. We decided to become roommates and move in with each other as soon as we could.

The next day I will never forget. We texted each other and asked, "So are we really going to do this?" And we both said, "*Yes!*" Three months later she and I found an apartment and moved in together.

We were both very clean people and liked having nice things, so we knew this was going to be a great relationship. She wasn't creeped out that I was a funeral director going to mortuary school. Both of us were excited to be living in a new apartment as friends. Little did we know we were going to go through a life-changing experience within the first month of being roommates.

The weekend of Elisabeth's birthday I was off work and we decided to go on an adventure; then meet up with all the girls for dinner and drinks. We went to the lake, found a stranded paddleboat, hopped in, and floated around for a while. We felt like rebels. We had no idea what we were doing. All we knew was we were having fun! We came home and had the girls over for dinner then headed out to paint the town red.

We had a blast. I had to be up the next morning to meet my family for church. Elisabeth was going to join us. We were tired but started getting ready for service at 11:00. I was in the kitchen while Elisabeth showered. I heard a really loud thump coming from the bathroom. I ran in and asked if she was okay. Elisabeth said she fell but was fine. I figured she was tired and slipped.

I returned to the kitchen then heard another thump.

Elisabeth was on the floor trying to get up. I asked what was going on and why she was falling? She said, "I am having these glitches and think I'm just tired and need to lay down." I helped her up and brought some water.

Elisabeth dropped the cup and fell to the floor with her eyes rolled back. I had no idea what was happening.

I moved Elisabeth on her side and away from the wall she hit with her head. I was yelling, "Can you hear me, what's wrong?" She started convulsing, her face was turning blue, blood was coming out of her mouth, and I was scared. Thank God her phone was within arm's reach. I called 9-1-1. I was yelling at the operator that I didn't know what to do; I was scared my roommate was about to die in my arms. I described what Elisabeth was doing. The operator told me she was having a grand mal seizure and keep her on her side—they'd send an ambulance immediately. I was praying to God for help, and for Elisabeth not to die. She stopped convulsing, fell into a deep sleep, then woke up frightened. The ambulance arrived. She had no idea what happened. We both were crying and scared. The ambulance took her to the hospital while I followed. I called my parents in tears and didn't know what else to do.

The doctor said Elisabeth wouldn't be able to drive, work, or go to school for a while. They were going to do lots of tests to diagnose her seizure. Although this was her first seizure, the doctor said she may have had others before but didn't realize it. Elisabeth was terrified to be alone. I stayed with her at the hospital—Elisabeth's family in Humboldt had been notified.

I went to gather a few of her things from the apartment and broke down. There was blood on the floor, which I frantically cleaned up. I have never been so scared for someone's life. I've dialed 9-1-1 before but this was the first time I thought I was going to witness someone I knew die in my arms. I have been around death all my life and met with many bereaved families, but I have never held someone who's possibly dying. I developed greater respect for nurses, paramedics, and firefighters that day. Elisabeth made a fast recovery. Her family came to see her for a couple days—she needed that.

Licensed Funeral Director

ELISABETH WAS GEARING up to graduate and I was preparing for license tests. I studied hard—secluding myself for a couple months to focus. I had to complete the national tests to graduate from my program. Towards the end of the program we took a practice test. I did well and felt prepared.

After passing all my classes with a seventy-six percent or better, I was qualified to take the nationals. National is a two-part test, about one hundred and fifty questions each, covering science and arts. State tests are next. The national tests are the hardest. I took the arts first, followed by science the next day. I knew the arts were going to be a struggle. I was told the arts section heavily covered laws, not just in the funeral industry but other industries. I decided to take the test in Redding and stay with Aunt Connie while I studied.

I was tested in an isolation room. They locked up my purse and checked my pockets to make sure I didn't have anything prohibited. It felt like I was checking into jail. I didn't know taking a funeral directors national test involved so much security. I sat in a small cubical between two other cubes. I felt uneasy about the questions halfway through the test. They were harder than expected. When finished, all I had to do was push the button and find out whether I passed or not.

I pushed the button. The results said … *Not Passed*. I was right below the percentile needed for passing—I was devastated. I called my parents and told Mom I didn't pass the arts section. She thought I was kidding at first, but my silence told her I wasn't joking. Both parents got on the phone and consoled me. There was still the science part to take the next day. They assured me it'll be okay and keep my head held high.

I went to Aunt Connie's and cried a little more. She took me out for dinner. The hard part for me was I excelled in school and had a high GPA. I was mystified why I didn't do well on the arts portion. I felt like a failure.

I studied more that night and felt ready for the science portion. I went into the same isolation room and was nervous all over again. My confidence level had dropped a little, so I tried to stay calm and collected. This time I felt a lot more confident with my answers. I pushed the same button, closed my eyes, and the word *Pass* popped up. Thank God. I was happy and felt much better. I passed with flying colors. I called my family, who were ecstatic. First Connie celebrated with me; then I went home for another celebration.

Having completed the nationals, I was qualified to graduate from the program and receive my degree in mortuary science. Family and friends attended graduation in Sacramento. I felt so good, though I still had to take the state funeral directors test and state embalmers test.

Taking the funeral directors test in Redding, I was put in the same isolation room as before; I had four hours to finish. The test was all on computer. They gave me earplugs if I wanted to use them. I was nervous like before, recalling the results of my arts test. I hoped this would be different. Two hours later, all I had to do was push results and find out if I was a funeral director or not. I prayed nervously. I pushed results and *Pass* came up! Woohooo. I was so happy; I immediately called my parents at work and shouted, "I am a funeral director now!" I received a document saying passed and a license number to practice in the state of California. I was overjoyed with the completion of my dedication and hard work. It paid off.

Lastly, the licensed embalmer test. I was sick of tests by then, but this was my final one—I was ready to be finished. I brought a friend with me. I knew this test wasn't going to take long and I wanted someone there to celebrate with. We drove to Sacramento. She shopped while I took the test. I pushed the results button one more time: *Pass*. Thankful I was finished, I called my parents yet again to tell them the good news. I added licensed embalmer to my list of credentials. My friend and I celebrated with lunch and shopping.

Graduation was over. I was now working at my dad's funeral home as a fully licensed employee. I walked into work with my head held a little higher that day and I didn't feel conceited doing it!

I was starting a new chapter of my life. Elisabeth moved out of town to another school. I moved into a new apartment in Chico on my own, and felt good about life.

MY GRANDFATHER (DAD's dad) died before I was born

from a heart attack the day after he retired from Rainbow Bread Company. I heard wonderful stories about Grandfather Newton, and how gracious he was. Grandfather Newton was buried in Chico Cemetery next to our funeral home about thirty years ago. My grandmother planned to be buried beside him.

Grandmother's second husband died in 2005 and was placed in our mausoleum. Grandmother wanted Grandfather Newton moved from Chico Cemetery to the mausoleum. Her plan was to be placed next to the both husbands upon death. I was curious how this was going to happen. Dad told me sometimes families return years later and want their loved one moved from one cemetery to another. The more I worked at the funeral home, the more I learned there is no weird way of dealing with death. Everyone is different and judgment should never be cast on them.

Dad helped unearth his father's casket after thirty years of burial. The casket was sent to our funeral home where Dad's business partner Bob opened it to see if he could retrieve Grandfather Newton's wedding ring. Sure enough, the wedding ring was there. Bob said Grandfather Newton still looked like himself even after thirty years of being under ground.

Dad didn't want to see his deceased father in that condition. However, I was curious. I asked Dad if could see Grandfather Newton and help get him ready for placement in the crypt. It wasn't easy seeing him in the old casket. His was the first excavated body I had seen and it'll probably be my last.

My sisters and I bought a long gold chain to hang the ring. We asked if we could take turns wearing the necklace. Dad was honored we wanted to. My sisters and I still wear

Grandfather Newton's ring around our necks.

Even though we never had the chance to meet him, Grandpa Newton is part of our daily life.

ANSWERING PHONES AT the funeral home, I received solicitations from nonprofit organizations and various advertisers. I forwarded them to Dad or Bob, wondering what kind of advertising we were being asked to buy, and were we involved with any organizations? I found out we're involved in many.

Dad always stressed the importance of our community role, whether it's being involved with a church, charity, club, or even bowling league. Since we were born and raised in Chico, Dad and I know many local people. We support their groups when possible. Dad has taken my sisters and me to events since childhood.

After becoming a full-time employee at the funeral home I quickly learned how crucial it was to help support the community and get involved. One such cause is Every Fifteen Minutes. Every other year, the Chico community gets the high schools together to build support for students against drunk driving. (Someone in the U.S. dies from a drunken driver every fifteen minutes.) The Fire Department, hospital, paramedics, and the funeral home get involved with the event, creating a very intense scene at one of the schools.

Dad assigned me and a couple other funeral directors to work with the schools and help any way we could. Thirty students became involved by acting—five of them as victims of a staged car accident. The remaining students came to school the day of the accident with their faces painted white. They couldn't talk with other students because they were "dead." A demolished upside down car was set on the football field. The five students in the faux car accident were acting drunk. One of them died; the driver was handcuffed, arrested, and driven away in the back seat of a patrol car; the other three were injured.

Another director and I headed to the accident to simulate an actual removal. All students, who had been let out of class, were standing on the sidelines. The Fire Department was there—paramedics were just leaving by ambulance with the injured students—red lights flashing. Adding to the drama, instead of bringing the removal van we normally use (a nice white Honda van), we pulled up in a hearse to reinforce the message of the staged tragedy. We got out and spoke to the police officers who told us what happened. We removed the gurney, gently placed the dead student onto it, and slid him in the hearse. He was taken to the funeral home, given a tour, and shown the process we use in actual death cases. During this time, parents of the students received calls from the officers who broke the news of either the death or injury of their child due to a car accident.

After the accident scene was cleared, the school held an assembly for students and facility to debrief on what happened. Guests speakers who knew or loved someone that died in a drunken driver accident recounted their experiences. Representatives from our funeral home, counselors, students, and paramedics also spoke.

We believe the Every Fifteen Minutes program has become a life-changing event. Every high school needs to partake in a program like this.

Infant Deaths

EXCITING THINGS WERE starting to happen. I had new business cards printed now that I had my license numbers, which we posted on our website. I was proud of myself and relieved knowing my schooling was done and I could advance my career in funeral services. I was working Monday through Friday from about eight till five. Every day was different. Working at a funeral home, you don't know what your day is going to bring you. You could be slow for one day, and then get five calls the next. You are always on your toes. I liked not having the same routine every day. I wasn't sitting at my desk all the time, nor was I on my feet all the time either.

Every fourth weekend I was the funeral director on call, which means that Friday after 5:30 p.m. when our office hours closed, the phones were turned over to me. I needed to be prepared all weekend for any removals, funerals, embalming, cremations, and remain available to meet with families. As the funeral director on call, you can't make plans with friends or family.

AFTER BECOMING FULLY licensed, I felt like I was just getting started in the funeral profession. I completed my apprenticeship and could now tell families I was a licensed funeral director and embalmer. I will never forget one particular day. ...

I received a call from the hospital that an infant had died and it was time for me to receive little Erica and transfer her to the funeral home. I had never met with a family whose baby died and I knew this was going to be very difficult. I brought a white blanket into the hospital to wrap the child. With an infant, we don't have to use an adult-size gurney—the funeral director can hold the baby instead. I went to the nurses' station and let them know I was from the funeral home to receive Erica. The nurse told me the family didn't want to let their baby go.

Fifteen family members stared at me when I walked into their room. Never before had I felt so uncomfortable. I didn't know what to say. I remember thinking: they do *not* teach you this in school, this is something I have to learn on my own. I introduced myself and explained when they were ready (which no one really ever is) I would carefully receive their baby girl and transfer her to the funeral home where we could all meet and make arrangements.

Erica's mother, crying softly, was holding her lifeless baby against her chest. She told me she didn't want to let her daughter go. I told her this does *not* have to be the last time she sees her little girl. I laid the white blanket on the bed. The mother laid the baby on it and wrapped her. I was holding back tears as I said, "I will take good care of your little baby." Both parents kissed their daughter's head, then I left the room with their dead baby daughter in my arms.

Driving back to the funeral home with this beautiful

baby girl, I started to cry. This was the first time I talked to parents in a hospital about making arrangements for their newborn. It wasn't the first time I cried with a family, but this was the first time that I really felt pain for a family. Babies are not supposed to die and parents are not supposed to bury their own children.

When someone dies, whether in a hospital, care home, or at home; within twenty-four hours a funeral home, according to California law, is to place the deceased into refrigeration or the body must be embalmed. (The purpose is to help slow decomposition.) This was the first time I had difficulty placing anyone into our refrigeration. I did not feel right placing a little baby in there; but it had to be done.

The next day the family of little Erica was coming in to talk about arrangements. The parents were accompanied by many family members supporting them through this difficult time. Even though I was now this licensed funeral director and embalmer, there was nothing during the arrangement that could help make things easier for them. They were too hurt by Erica's unexpected death.

A lot of times when I meet with the average family I laugh with them, listen to great stories, look at photos, and arrange a celebration of life service for their loved one. However, when meeting with a family who is going through an unexpected, sudden, or accidental death, there is usually none of that.

The family wanted to have a viewing for their little Erica so friends and family could come and see her one last time, and they wanted to have her buried in the cemetery. At our funeral home, when we have an infant death, we do our services pro bono. We try to help as much as we can with our services. I asked the family if I could get permission to embalm Erica because it would help with having a viewing. They agreed. I told the mother I would be the one to care for her little body. That's when the mother told me that when I came to the hospital the other day, she felt more comfortable having another woman taking her baby away from her. She told me how much better she felt knowing I would be the one to treat Erica's little body. I told the parents they could dress their little girl if they wanted, which they did. Most parents who go through the death of a child want to be the ones who dress them and place them in the small casket. I like to give them the option every time.

Although I was now licensed with enough experience to feel comfortable in the prep room, nothing prepared me for having to embalm a baby. I remember, as a child, Dad talking about helping families who lost a baby. He told me it was one of the hardest parts of the job—especially the necessary preparation of their tiny bodies. I asked Dad to come into the prep room while I embalmed Erica. He was there more for moral support—I knew how to embalm an infant, but I did not like it. He told me all funeral directors struggle with this and it's very common to feel the way I was.

After the embalming, I felt exhausted from all the emotions I was going through. I had become good at trying to separate myself from my families I had been serving. Dad told me something that will carry with me the rest of my life, "You need to professionally separate yourself from your families." Sometimes it's difficult—I connect with my families on an emotional level. And that's healthy, for the most part.

Following Erica's funeral, I wanted a break. We have five

other funeral directors and embalmers at our funeral home. When one of our directors meets with a deceased infant's family, an unexpected, or a sudden death, the director takes a break from those cases so he or she doesn't get too over-whelmed. I could not be a funeral director exclusively—it's too much sometimes. That's why I also wanted to become an embalmer, so I could have balance in my job.

THIS NEW CAREER was my life, but I was working so hard and so much that I came home exhausted, enjoyed a glass of wine, and went to bed. I was growing up fast and having a hard time accepting it. I was twenty-three and handling emotional situations everyday.

I wrote earlier how important it was for funeral direc-tors to professionally separate themselves from the families they meet with or they could burn out. The more I met with families, the more I learned how to serve them and not involve myself emotionally at the same time. I have compassion for the families I meet—I care for my families. Then there was this family. ...

I was on call Sunday afternoon at my apartment cleaning and doing laundry. The cell phone ringer was set on loud in case I got a call from the answering service. It had been a quiet weekend for the most part, so I attended church that day and spent some time with my family afterwards. The phone rang and caller ID displayed *answering service*. I stopped what I was doing and answered, ready to talk to a family or leave for a removal. The answering service said a grandfather was on the line wanting to speak to a funeral director and know the process for helping his daughter who lost her baby sons in Redding. I told the service to patch him through. I sat down at the kitchen table with a pad of paper, preparing myself for a difficult conversation.

Tom told me his daughter was at a Redding hospital. She gave birth to twin boys about eight months ago. They both died that morning. My heart sank and went out to the family. Tom's voice sounded fairly young. I had an idea his daughter was close to my age. Sure enough, Tom told me his daughter was only thirty and she and her husband were elated she finally became pregnant. They had been trying to have a baby many years. Five months after birth their pediatrician diagnosed the twins with a rare muscle dysfunction.

Tom told me his daughter is afraid of how her little boys will be handled and wanted to make sure they were properly cared for. I told him I would be the one handling her little boys and would hold and care for them as if they were my own. Tom wanted to proceed—we could come to the hospital to receive the twins.

I decided to drive to the hospital, eighty miles away, meet his daughter, and pick up the babies. She could hold her little boys on the drive to Chico, and I'd drive her back to Redding. As I pulled into the hospital, my heart saddened. I had been on infant removals before, and I had met with infant families before, but I felt specially connected to this family on an emotional level, even though I had only spoken to the grandfather on the phone.

I brought two baby blankets in case they were needed to wrap the babies. The nursing supervisor led me into the small room where I met Tom, his daughter, his son-in-law, and the two beautiful twin boys. Tom introduced himself, thanked me for being there, and said they were ready to go. Danielle (Tom's daughter) asked if it was okay for her dad to ride with us to Chico. I told her sure.

Her husband needed to stay at the hospital and did not want to join us. He kissed his sons' foreheads, looked at me and said, "Please, take good care of my little boys." I teared up and told him I would. The ride to Chico was nearly silent except I could hear Tom and his daughter crying the entire way. I felt so bad for the family. It's times like these that make you wonder: *why?* Why does something this awful have to happen? During difficult times I rely on my faith in God. I pray and give my concerns to Him. Even for those with faith, one can ask why?

At the funeral home, I gave Danielle papers to take and review with her husband. We would meet the next day. Danielle asked if this was the last time she was going to see her little boys. It did not have to be the last time. I told her when she comes the next day she can visit her sons before cremation. Danielle handed me her babies, looked at me and said, "Thank you for your compassion." The little boys in my arms looked so alive and healthy. They were beautiful. I was sad how soon they were taken from Earth. I prayed for the family silently, went into my office, and shut the door for a while to be alone and regroup.

The next day Danielle came in with her dad and mother-in-law who was unable to see the babies at the hospital. Danielle returned the signed paperwork and brought her own urns for me to put the cremated remains. She asked to see her little boys one more time. I brought the twins into the viewing room and she held them for the last time. I left the room to let the family say goodbye in privacy. ...

Tom entered my office and said they were ready for me. This is where I lost it. I sat down with Danielle and told her I know this is hard for her. I wanted her to know I was going to take sweet care of her little boys; I was going to be gentle and treat them as if they were my own. Danielle handed me her babies. In tears, she said something to me I will *never* forget: "You will be a wonderful mother some-day." I began to cry. I was sitting with the family. Danielle kissed her babies and said she couldn't believe she only got to spend eight months with her newborn. We all sat in the room crying while I held the deceased twins.

Died of a Broken Heart

I TOOK TIME off from meeting with unexpected/sudden death families for the week following Erica's and the twins' funerals. I still met with families that week, but was careful which families to avoid burnout. One of the families I selected turned into a new experience.

I was told people could die from a broken heart. I really didn't understand what that meant … until I became a funeral director. I went on a removal with my dad. Joyce lost her husband of sixty years. He was under hospice care; his heart had been failing for quite some time. Joyce said she had been expecting the death. Their children and grandchildren had just visited, coming together as a family one last time. It was time to celebrate his life and she wanted to plan a really nice funeral for him. Dad and I wheeled in the gurney and asked if she was okay with us going ahead and gently placing her husband on it. Joyce agreed. She told us she has been ready for this a while, and was glad he wasn't suffering anymore.

We placed her husband on the gurney and allowed his face to be exposed atop a soft pillow for her last kiss. That meant a lot to Joyce. She said she feared the part when we came to remove his body. She leaned over her husband, kissed him on the forehead, and wiped a couple tears away. Joyce was assured we would take good care of him and when she was ready we would go over the arrangements.

We held his funeral a couple days later. The military came to his gravesite (this time I was prepared for the gun salute) and folded the American flag, which they handed Joyce. After the funeral, I said my goodbyes to Joyce and told her if she ever needed anything I would be there for her. She thanked me and we went our own ways. I mailed Joyce a copy of her husband's obituary that I laminated and thought she would appreciate.

Two weeks later I was on call. The answering service reported a removal in Chico. Joyce had died. I couldn't believe it. I was just with her a couple weeks ago, how could she have died so soon? She seemed healthy! I went to the house I had just been a few weeks ago for her husband. Her adult children, whom I met at their dad's funeral, were there. They were comforted to see me at her home. Joyce died at her kitchen table playing solitaire. Next to her cards was the letter I had written her along with the laminated obituary hanging next to the table. I thought to myself, Joyce died of a broken heart.

Passed out Nurse

EVERY MORNING AROUND 8:30 all the funeral directors gather to go over the board, just like doctors and nurses do in the hospital. We talk about what we are going to be doing that day and who's going to be with what family and who will be in charge of the prep room, embalming, and cremations. This particular morning my dad wrote there was going to be a nursing tour at the funeral home.

Getting through mortuary school has been compared to going through nursing school. Both require the same amount of schooling and the classes are similar.

I have many friends who are or will soon be nurses. When they went through their program while I was in mortuary school we compared classes, studied together, and talked about the different situations we experienced. Being a nurse, the hope is you don't see death, and everyone who enters the hospital will leave the hospital—alive. However, many times that's not the case and the nurse sees death firsthand. With that in mind, many local nursing instructors have asked if our funeral home would be willing to give tours to their students. We've jumped on board with the requests.

I asked Dad if I could give the tour that day. I hadn't

done one before. He didn't argue—he was hoping I'd ask. I love to get in front of people and speak; public speaking is a passion of mine. Whenever I have the chance to get up and hold a microphone I seize the opportunity. Little did I know this tour was going to be different than I imagined.

Showing up were nursing students of all ages, a larger group than usual. Before I began with the tour and discussion, I announced, as Dad suggested, we would be going into the prep room and if anyone felt uncomfortable, they didn't have to go in. I wondered to myself, what nurse is going to be uncomfortable in a prep room? They will be working in a hospital with all sorts of instruments, blood, odors, and sickness.

I knew many students questioned why they needed to tour a funeral home and what the significance was. With that in mind, I started off in our chapel and discussed why it is necessary for them to see the process of death and to be prepared: sometime during their profession, they will come across the death of a patient. I gave them a brief history of our funeral home, from taking over the previous owner to all the different funerals we have been involved in. I love interaction; so I encouraged questions along the way and boy did I get questions. It was great. The students were interacting with me talking about the process of death and what we do as funeral directors and embalmers.

We moved from the chapel into our viewing room, which are connected by French doors. I explained the room is used mainly for open casket viewings. It's a comfortable room with couches, chairs, and proper lighting. We also use the room for a reception area. Many funerals are a celebration and the families want food and drinks after the service. We can provide that for them.

After the viewing/reception room I walked the students into our garage area where we have the refrigeration unit. When we come back from removals we log in the deceased and place them in refrigeration. I could tell some of the students were getting a little uncomfortable knowing they were getting closer to entering the prep room. In the garage area is our crematory as well, and I took the students over to it and explained a little about cremation. More questions were arising now that we were talking about the care of the bodies and what can be done after death for disposition. I answered questions like, how long does it take to cremate someone? (about two hours), is there an odor? (no odor while cremation is occurring), do you cremate more than one person at a time? (legally not allowed), can the families watch the cremation? (yes, families may watch), and how hot does the temperature get? (1400–1800 degrees). These are all great questions a crematory operator is frequently asked.

From the crematory area I told the students we were about to go into the prep room and those feeling uncomfortable could wait in the chapel for the others to finish the tour. They all said they felt comfortable and wanted to go in the prep room. I prepared the students before we entered—there were no bodies in there, there will be a sterile smell (which they should be used to), and I had instruments out for them to see, as well as the different chemicals we use during an embalming.

We gathered inside and I began talking about the process of embalming. Ten minutes into my talk, I noticed a girl was looking a pale and nauseated. I stopped and asked if she needed to step outside or wanted water or something. She looked at me then wobbled her knees and passed out in the middle of the prep room floor. The students around her had broken her fall. Her professor walked her outside. I was stunned; I did not think I would ever see a nurse pass out in a prep room. I felt badly for her. After that I asked if anyone else felt sick or needed to go outside. Everyone said they were just fine.

The students asked many questions in the prep room, mainly about embalming and autopsies. I enjoyed educating them. Their questions included: how long does it take to embalm someone? (about two hours for the average person, and about four hours on someone who has had an autopsy), how much chemical do you inject? (about eight quarts of chemicals), how many vessels do you raise? (depends on the person, usually you inject in the right common carotid and drain out the right jugular vein, but if the embalmer does not see signs of distribution throughout the entire body, then the embalmer needs to raise the appropriate vessels sectionally), and what kind of instruments do embalmers use? (same instruments doctors use).

I led the tour into our memories room where sample urns and casket corners are displayed to show families. I told the students that we, as funeral directors, take the families into the memories room after or during the arrangement so they family can see the different options for burial or cremation. Lastly, I took them into the mausoleum where we also take families to show them the option for entombment.

Giving nursing students the tour helped me realize how much we are a death-denying society. Even nurses who are in the medical field don't like to talk about it too much. However, after the tour I asked if it helped them in any way, or shed another light on death. They all agreed—yes to both!

Unrecognizeable

OUR FAMILY HAS travelled to the Pacific Coast a couple times each year staying in a cabin for a week. We enjoyed escaping the Sacramento Valley summer heat that sometimes reaches triple digits for days, and cooling off on the rugged beaches around Fort Bragg in northern California. Who doesn't like the beach? We've been doing this since

Destiny and Shawntel spread cremated remains from boat at Fort Bragg

I can remember. Dad would scatter ashes out at sea as we watched until we were old enough to help. These trips are special memories my sisters and I share with our parents. We still try to head west over the Coastal Range Mountains even though we're busier.

Recently, after our family returned from Fort Bragg, I received a frantic phone call. Kate, a friend of mine, said a friend of hers died in a car accident two days ago and she didn't know where his body was taken and what to do. I had to calm her down and start from the beginning before I could help. The first thing I asked Kate was where did Sam die so I could call the coroner's office.

Kate told me everything she heard from the news and Internet. Sam and Carla had driven to Mendocino County, the same area our family vacationed, to celebrate their first anniversary. On their way back to Chico, a semitruck over-corrected and sideswiped their car, causing it to flip into the embankment and roll. Sam died in the driver's seat. Carla was pinned in the passenger's seat semiconscious. Paramedics rushed her away from the scene. Kate didn't know where either was taken.

Kate soon found out Carla was in Chico—Carla's neighbor had seen her being dropped off by a taxi—and Carla had locked herself in her home! Kate went over there; Carla let her in. We found out Carla had been taken to a Mendocino hospital. Her injuries were visible all over her body. She said she left the hospital without permission. She wanted to go home. She had taken a five-hour cab ride home, alone!

I knew asking about Sam was not going to be easy on Carla. Her eyes were swollen from the accident and tears. I knew there could be denial with what happened. I went online and searched Mendocino County news. The first thing that popped up was the car accident. I read the story then called the coroner's office and explained I am a funeral director in Chico and would be taking care of the family. I wanted as much information as possible to start arrangements.

The coroner told me they performed an autopsy and Sam was being transferred to a local funeral home. I called the local funeral home and told them I was heading over to transfer Sam back to Chico. I needed a signed release from Carla. I called Kate to let her know I located Sam's body and everything would be taken care of. She called Carla.

With Carla's signed papers in hand, I left to bring Sam back home to Chico. I called Carla when I returned. Sam was now in our care. Carla could discuss the arrangements with me at the funeral home or I would be glad to meet at her house. She was very sweet with me on the phone and felt meeting me at the funeral home would be just fine. Before she arrived, I went into our refrigeration to see Sam's body.

Since Sam was in a car accident and had an autopsy, his body was not going to be in good shape—most likely unrecognizable. I opened the body bag and looked around. Before closing the bag, I saw something shine. I found his wedding ring! I cleaned the ring and placed it in a baggie to give Sam's wife.

I began to prepare myself to talk with Carla. I was afraid I was going to say the wrong thing, or I wanted so badly to be able to say the *right* thing. There is no special word, but I was wishing there was. Sam's wife came in alone. My mom was there to greet her at the door and lead her to the arrangement office. I brought in a warm cup of coffee and sat next to her at the table. My heart was beating rapidly. I began telling her I was also a good friend of Kate and as soon as Kate had called me I did my best to help in any way possible. I asked Carla if she wanted to talk to me about what happened and, sure enough, Carla started to tell me the story of seeing her husband killed in the car accident.

They were coming back from their anniversary and Sam chose to drive because Carla was tired. When the semitruck ran into their car, Carla saw everything in slow motion and remembered their car rolling down a hill. Once it stopped rolling she looked at her husband in the driver's seat and knew he was dead. She proceeded to describe being stuck in the car next to her husband's body, unable to move. After the fire department came, she forgot the rest until she woke up in the hospital. At this point I was trying not to let her see me crying.

I, again, did not know what to say to her. I was shocked with the story and felt awful for her. There is no right/wrong way to grieve. Sam's wife told me she was glad he was in Chico and we were taking care of his body. She wanted him cremated and would take his cremated remains home. She did not want to see him—just wanted him cremated soon. Had she wanted to see him, knowing his body was unrecognizable, I would have shown her his hand, or a part of his body that was recognizable and cover the rest of his body with a sheet. She said the last image she is going to live with for the rest of her life is her husband dead in their car seat next to her.

I told Carla I recovered his wedding ring and knew it was not going to change the horrific image she has of her husband, but she could always cherish the memories they shared together and their marriage. She took the ring and cried on my shoulder.

AFTER MEETING WITH Sam's wife and trying to help her join a support group of others who've gone through similar tragedies, I was learning more about how everyone grieves differently. I was sure Carla would have wanted to see Sam's hand before cremation because that's what I would have wanted to do. Despite the fact he had been in an accident, I think I'd want to see my husband one more time. However, for Sam's wife, her decision was healthy for her. All options were presented to her and she did what was best for her. Our job as funeral directors is to give families options. I met with another widow who had her own way of grieving.

ON ONE OF my nights on call the answering service phoned and said they had the Sheriff's Department on the line and wanted an ETA (estimated time of arrival) from us. There was a very bad accident and make sure I brought a body pouch. I called another funeral director to meet me at the office and join me on the call. It was about two in the morning; pouring rain. All I knew was it was a bad car accident and involved a young man. Upon arrival, we saw his car had flipped over a fence and rolled many times into someone's front yard. The car was completely smashed. I knew I was about to see an unrecognizable body.

Three sheriff's deputies approached and directed me to park the removal van on the front lawn near the car. We removed the gurney from the van and took out the body bag. Half of the young man's body was in the car and the other half on the ground. I had never seen something like this. It was my first car accident call involving an unrecognizable body. There was a strong smell of alcohol around the car. Apparently the young man was going about 85 mph and spun out of control in the rain; rolled into the fence, and died upon impact.

The deputies told me he had a wife and minor children. I jotted down as much information as I could, then transferred the mutilated body to the funeral home. The next morning at 8:30 I was at work reviewing the information. I told the other funeral directors and staff his body is not viewable and we will be hearing from his wife sometime that day to go over arrangements.

Around 9:00 A.M. we were called by the frantic wife who was in denial that her husband died. She demanded to see him right away. This is a normal reaction—a family in denial about an accidental death and wants to view the body for proof it happened. It's completely understandable. I asked the wife to come to the funeral home and we would talk over things. She arrived, rightfully hysterical, with her children. I sat her down and explained I had been on the call and was at the accident scene and, due to the circumstances; her husband's body was not viewable or recognizable. This was not a concern to the widow; she demanded to see her husband despite the condition of his body. As a funeral director I wanted to prepare her for what she was about to see, and that I was only going to expose his hands. I also told her he has a tattoo on his left hand and she would be able to see it. I asked my dad to come into the prep room and help me place the young man's body on a dressing table, take his hands out of the body bag, and cover the rest with a sheet.

We placed him in our viewing room and I went into the arrangement office where the widow was pacing back and forth. I took her into the viewing room while her children stayed behind with her sister. I told her I would remain in the room with her if she wanted (also, I wanted to make sure that she did not pull down the sheet). She entered the viewing room and started screaming. I shut the door behind us. She walked over to her husband's body and touched his cold hands. She pointed out the tattoo on his left hand and whispered, "This is my husband." I told her to take her time. She turned to me and explained what happened the night of the accident.

Her husband had been out drinking because of a family argument and she hadn't heard anything about him until a phone call from the Sheriff's Department around 4:00 A.M. I assured the widow we were going to take good care of her husband and would help honor him with a funeral and provide a place for family and friends to gather, share stories, and, most importantly, provide a place for them to come and grieve. She thanked me for my honesty about his condition and for allowing her to at least see her husband's hands.

The family needed reassurance he died. She said she could grieve properly now that she knew it was her husband. Her grieving process began after the touch of a hand.

Never Forget

BEFORE YOU READ my last funeral arrangement story, I want to say being a funeral director has its rewards. The stories I have shared are difficult and hard, but also rewarding. I am with families during one of the *most* crucial times during their life and guide them through not only funeral arrangements, but also the healing process.

I was on call for the weekend and had just finished working a funeral in our chapel. I was ready to lock up and head home. Then I received a phone call from the hospital: they needed me to be there right away. I was given no explanation. I showed up and five sheriff's cars were in front of the hospital. I went inside and asked the nurse what the situation was, and why were there so many squad cars? She said they were dealing with a child abuse case and Child Protective Services had been called. I was to transfer a dead little boy, Michael, to our funeral home.

The revelation shocked me; I had *never* dealt with an abuse case. I entered the room full of deputies and a five-year-old child lying dead on the bed. My heart dropped. I was speechless. I took Michael to the funeral home and waited, not knowing what to do next. Usually we have a next-of-kin to contact—a spouse or parent. In Michael's case, I didn't have any information. A caller from CPS told me Michael's parents were in jail and I was to do nothing until I heard more.

As soon as I hung up, a couple cars arrived. I stepped out and greeted them. They came to make arrangements for their nephew. I invited them inside. They started by telling me their little nephew had died. I put it together they were there for Michael. I was right. They identified themselves as his family.

I excused myself from the room so I could call my dad for support and help. He told me that out of all his forty years of being in the business, he had never dealt with a fatal abuse case. There were laws we needed to look into and must be careful we do things accordingly. Who had the right of disposition? How long until the parents go to court? How do I make these arrangements? All these questions were going through our heads. Dad suggested I go back in, talk with the family and gather information about Michael to encourage the process.

I didn't delve into detail; I wanted them to feel comfortable and safe. They said Michael's parents were in jail and weren't sure when they'd be released to help with arrangements. I knew nothing about the parents other than they were involved with CPS. The aunt and uncle continued, telling me the boy's parents were under suspicion for child abuse. Immediately, walls went up for me. I felt a little uneasy. After giving me more information, I said I'd give them a call on Monday when I expected to hear from Child Protective Services. There wasn't much I could do until then. The family asked if there would be an autopsy. I said most likely because of the circumstances. They understood.

I went over to my parents after work and discussed the

situation. I admitted I was really uncomfortable during the arrangement and hoped the family didn't notice. The next day the Sunday morning paper carried a front-page story about Michael. His parents were jailed on charges of child abuse and due in court weeks later. Now that the story was public, I speculated we were going to be bombarded by people who wanted more information.

I updated the staff about Michael the next day, Monday. Phones started ringing off the hook. Friends, relatives, and the public in general wanted to know what happened to the little boy and was there going to be a funeral for him? We would not disclose any information until we heard more from the family.

The Sheriff's Department called and said the local pathologist was going to do an autopsy that day. I didn't want to assist because I was already having a hard time with the arrangements. The staff stepped in to help me with a few things concerning the Health and Safety Code pertaining to the arrangements and determining who was the direct next of kin if the parents were in jail. We never had a case like this, so we carefully made sure we were doing everything legally.

I learned, according to the Health and Safety Code, the parents still had rights to the disposition of their son's body until they were actually convicted of the crime. Michael's parents were charged with murder, but until they were convicted they still had rights. I gave their attorney an affidavit to assign their rights to Michael's aunt and uncle. After the parents signed the papers I moved forward with the family, completed more paperwork, and made decisions.

The family wanted a funeral; along with an open casket viewing, followed by a burial at the cemetery. Michael's autopsy was invasive which would create a challenge for me as an embalmer to make him look presentable. The family signed authorization for embalming, along with all the other necessary paperwork.

Service was being planned for the next weekend. To help with safety and privacy, we thought it wise *not* to announce the date and time of service in the paper. All arrangements were finalized after I finished a four-hour meeting with the family going over details of the service. I assured them we were taking good care of their nephew and doing our best to make him look presentable in his little casket.

I will never forget entering the prep room where I normally feel confident. This day was different than most. I had never seen such an invasive autopsy on anyone. As an investigation of criminal abuse, it was protocol for the pathologist to explore all the evidence needed for conviction. Everything from his small hands down to his feet had to be examined. I felt sick to my stomach (as I write this I have the same feeling I had that day) and started to cry.

I was unable to do the embalming alone. Other employees stepped into the prep room to help me. I cannot describe the feelings an embalmer experiences when doing preparations for a child. We spent hours taking care of Michael—in silence most of the time. We went home feeling different—I know I did.

Calls came in hourly asking about the little boy. We were not told the parents' legal status and did not know if they would be allowed to attend their son's funeral. To be honest, I was praying they wouldn't because I knew if the public found out the parents were at the funeral it could become dangerous. Public response to the abuse was very strong. We didn't want more problems for the family. The police assigned an undercover cop to the service in case of trouble.

Since I was the funeral director working with the family, I was in charge, and took all the calls that came in. This was *not* easy on me. I wanted to help the family, I didn't want to get too involved in the situation, and I did not want to pass judgment on anyone or anything. I needed to focus on taking care of the relatives of Michael.

Michael's little casket was shipped to the funeral home. It was hard to look at it. Obviously, we see caskets day in and day out. However, we seldom see infant caskets (thank goodness).

The boy's aunt brought in clothes and a little baseball cap for him to wear. My dad and I dressed and placed him in his casket. I was pleased with the way he looked. We moved his little casket into our chapel and I remember just sitting there in a chair; not saying a word for a long time.

The entire staff helped me with the funeral that week-end. His brothers and sisters attended but his parents couldn't because of their court date. There was a lot of emotion in the packed chapel. I went up to the lectern and closed the service at the end. The family and I drove to the cemetery and privately buried the boy. On the drive back I told my dad I needed a couple days away from the funeral home and meeting with families. I was spent. Aside from the little boy, I was meeting with three other families (one of which I knew personally). I needed time away. My body was showing physical signs of stress. Dad agreed, and I took a long weekend off from the business of death.

Betty Jane

BETTY JANE COULD have not come at a better time. ...

After taking a nice long weekend away from the business of death, I felt refreshed and ready to start a new week. A message on my desk directed me to call one of the care homes for a meeting with an elderly woman named Betty Jane about her pre-arrangements. She had questions and was unable to drive so I brought along paperwork in case it was needed. She wanted to meet in the lobby of her modest apartment building. I asked, "where should I look for you" because I didn't know what she looked like. Betty Jane replied, "Honey, you'll know it's me because I am the only old lady with a black eye."

I could tell this was going to be an interesting meeting. I headed out to the care home, went into the lobby, and sure enough there was a woman with a black eye front and center at the table. I introduced myself and asked how did she get the black eye? Betty Jane said she fell out of bed and hit the nightstand. Betty Jane was very funny and blunt. "I am almost eighty-eight years old and this black eye is not going to stop me from having fun." I loved Betty Jane already. I knew she and I were going to get along great.

Betty Jane asked how I got into the funeral business. She

said I'm quite young to be doing such an "adult" job. I told her my story about the family business, my job came naturally, and I recently graduated from mortuary school. Betty Jane said she was a nurse many many years ago. She had two children, but her son had died years ago. We talked at length; almost forgetting why I was there in the first place. She told me my dad helped their family when her husband Frank died years ago, and how compassionate Ric was to her and the family. I was a lot like my dad, she said, and I would make a good funeral director and counselor. Betty Jane was full of life—she told me many stories. I wanted to continue our talk and promised I would call later to take her out for a glass of wine and dinner.

I returned to the funeral home a little more full of life that day. I had just enjoyed a three-hour conversation with a complete stranger and learned so much about her I couldn't wait to see her again and hear more stories. I picked Betty Jane up a few days later for dinner at an Italian restaurant. She ordered a glass of white wine and I ordered red. Betty Jane began talking about her nursing days and how things were so different when she was in her twenties compared to nursing today and the way hospitals are run now. She nursed wounded soldiers during World War II and met her husband then. She grew up poor, but her husband took care of her and their children fairly well. She took up painting while she was a stay-at-home mom. She asked if I ever watched the TV show, *Lassie*. I said yes, I loved it growing up. "Well," Betty nonchalantly said, "our dog played on that show. They used different 'lassie dogs' and ours was one of them." I was like, "W*hat?* That's crazy cool."

The waiter asked if we'd like another glass of wine. I said I was fine. Betty Jane looked at me and said, "Well, since someone is being a party-pooper, I guess I won't have one either." I started laughing and ordered another glass each.

Betty Jane was spunky. She asked if I wanted to see her sketches. Her talent hung throughout her apartment: mountains, flowers, instruments, animals, and people from years ago when she studied art. I said my favorite painting was the violin and sheet of music. I never played the violin, but her depiction was mesmerizing. She wanted me to meet her daughter, a retired professor at CSU, Chico. I agreed.

A week later the three of us were enjoying dinner and champagne at her daughter's house. Betty Jane had a surprise for me: a painting of a violin she created after our last visit. I loved it. I felt special owning one of her originals which was signed on the back, "Love, your eighty-eight-year-old friend, Betty." I have learned so much from her. The three of us still have dinner together. Always cherish your friendships. ... Cheers to all the Betty Jane's out there!

Check Please

AFTER READING ABOUT my work life, you may be wondering, what's the story about Shawntel's post-graduation *dating* life? Good question.

Now that I had a career, my own apartment, didn't have to commute to Sacramento, and my "boy issues" were in the past, I was open to dating.

My last relationship was with the marine, which didn't end well. Apparently I tend to pick real winners. I needed to make sure I went about this dating thing the right way. I was well aware of bright red flags now, and I knew what I did *not* want in a man.

I have amazing friends. However, they want to try setting me up with guys they know, or guys their boyfriends know, and they *think* they have found the right man for me. Most of the time things don't work out and I usually feel badly because my girlfriend was sure it was a perfect match. Take Madison for example. She and I have been friends for many years. She works for a doctor and sees a lot of people visiting the office. Madison told me about a promising guy who worked on some of their machines and seemed very nice.

I told her I'd like to meet him, which Madison was eager

to arrange. It was around Christmastime and we were celebrating a friend's birthday at a restaurant—a perfect setting for him to join us. His name is Ethan. He was about thirty. (perfect age for me). Ethan entered and Madison introduced us. He was polite and seemed sweet. To be honest, I was not attracted to him right away, but I am all about giving someone a chance.

Ethan left to buy me a glass of red wine, came back over to me, and put his arm around my lower back. I was thinking to myself, ummm what is going on here? I slyly moved away from him; Ethan followed. I hardly spoke two words to Ethan before he thought it must be okay to put his arm around a complete stranger. I know I was new to dating, but this was *not* normal. Was he already marking his territory? No no no no, not okay. The entire night he tried being by my side. People were even asking if he was with me or not. I told Madison about the questions. She laughed with me and apologized, "Well, I didn't see that coming." Let's just say my *red* flag was waving in front of my face that night.

MY PROFESSION IS not like the usual jobs most people are comfortable with. So when it comes to dating and I talk to a guy about some of the passions in my life and what I do, if I see the big bubble above his head I'm thinking, *check please.*

Here's an example of said bubble. I met a man at a social. Bill was an insurance salesperson who recently graduated from Sacramento State. I had lived in Sacramento for a couple years and thought things would go good if we went on a date. He invited me out to dinner. Bill had no idea about my job and that I work around death. I knew the evening was going to be interesting. I had no experience explaining myself to a guy that I was interested in because I had only been in a couple relationships, and they were before I became a funeral director/embalmer.

Bill took me to a nice restaurant and we began talking about life and the things we enjoy. Then he asked, "What is it that you do?" I took a deep breath, a big gulp of red wine, and said, "I am a funeral director and embalmer." Bill's face turned another shade of white. Then it was his turn to take a *big* gulp of wine. He adjusted his collar and I think he was at a loss for words, or stunned because he really didn't say much after that. I went on to tell him briefly about how I got into the profession. Not wanting to freak him out too much, I was very soft with my words.

I know how most people feel and think about the funeral profession. I have dealt with this stigma my entire life. Heck, I used to be one of those who thought it was weird and that's why I wouldn't tell people what my dad did for a living. I've been thankful Dad found my mom and she wasn't repulsed by my dad's profession. Cheers to you, Mom!

Bill didn't ask a lot of questions about my job, which is understandable to some extent. I told him how difficult work can be and yet how rewarding it is. Bill proceeded: "So, you see dead people?" I knew right then this date was going no further than dinner ... the *check please* bubble went up! Bill took me home after dinner and we had the awkward goodbye of, "Call you sometime."

ANOTHER "DATE GONE wrong" or "check please" (on *my* part, this time) story was probably the most interesting date I had ever been on, including how we met.

At a restaurant, my two sisters noticed this good-looking guy eating by himself. They both looked at me with that look of ... go get 'im! I was thinking no way, I am not going to walk over to this stranger and ask if he's single. Plus, aren't women the ones who are suppose to be pursued, not the other way around? Both girls were eager for their older sister to find a man but that night they went a little overboard.

After dinner, Destiny decided to approach the tall, dark, and handsome man and ask him if he was single and would be interested in taking her older sister out on a date. I was mortified. I was sitting next to my parents with my head down in embarrassment. Remember, I don't turn red or get embarrassed except the time my pants ripped in mortuary school. Well, this was the second time I've turned red and was completely embarrassed.

Phil told Destiny he was single and would love to take me out on a date. He came over to me and politely asked for my phone number and said he would call and we could work it out to go to dinner or something.

After discretely yelling at both of my sisters for forcing this beautiful man upon me, I thought maybe this could be "the guy." From what I knew about him, he seemed very sweet, and he was *very* good looking. I call him tall, dark, and handsome, because that's exactly what he was.

Phil called that evening and said he wanted to take me to dinner before he left for a conference. Between my busy schedule and his, we were able to arrange an evening

Dinner went really well. Our conversation flowed. I still thought he was tall, dark, and handsome. He had a great job, was well rounded, loved Chico, and enjoyed going to church (bonus points). I was actually looking forward to seeing him again. I can usually tell on the first date if things are going to work out or not, and I tend to loose interest pretty quickly. However, my tall, dark, and handsome man was keeping my interest.

Let me just say, while I was dating, all my friends were getting engaged, moving in together, having babies, or already married. Why is it that once all your friends are in relationships you are the only single one left (you feel like the only one remaining on the entire planet) and you start feeling the need to get on the bandwagon and find someone quickly? ... Maybe that's why my dates all failed. If you rush it, things will get messy! Hmm, I think I just answered my own question. Back to tall, dark, and handsome.

Phil invited me to his house for a glass of red wine (my weakness) after he returned from the conference. He opened an expensive bottle and we began talking. Here's where things got weird—brace yourself.

Sisters Destiny, Shawntel and Vanessa Newton

As I was telling Phil about my workday he loudly passed gas, farted, tooted, ripped it, whatever you want to call it. I was completely speechless. This was our second date and he's already releasing bodily gasses in front of me? Yuck! I looked at him and said, "Excuse you." I was also laughing because you can't help but laugh when someone toots. Phil said he really didn't mean to let it out—it was an accident.

So being the girl who loves to give everyone the benefit of the doubt (as you know from reading this book), I decided it was best to let that slide and pretend nothing happened. Phil and I continued our conversation but I couldn't stop thinking about what just happened. I kid you not; five minutes later he did it again. Mind you, the air wasn't passing quietly, but loud, drawn out passings. I figured this was not an anomaly—he was simply a gassy man. Looking at Phil, I asked, "Okay, are you just comfortable in front of me, or are you just gassy?" Phil told me he was just a "gassy guy." Ewwww!

Needless to say, I left his house that night knowing gasman and I were not going to continue this "relationship." Our future was a huge *no no!*

That night I told my sisters what happened and they said well, so much for tall, dark, and handsome.

Are you feeling empathy for my dating life yet?

I MET A firefighter who was going to paramedic school. Women will agree with me on this: most firefighters are good looking—it's something about those uniforms that's irresistible. We met while I was out with my girlfriends. He knew some of them and stopped to say hi. Brody and I started talking about our jobs. After finding out I was a funeral director and embalmer he wanted to know if he could ask questions about my work because he's been on calls where he's seen death. I thought to myself … no bubble above the head; this is a good start. Finally, a good-looking man was asking me sincere questions about my job. Really? *Yes!*

In our small county, funeral directors are one of the first on the emergency call list along with the firefighters, paramedics, and Sheriff's Department. So my firefighter guy and I had a lot to relate to. We even found out we had been on some of the same calls.

Brody made me realize how much it meant to be with someone who was okay with my job and talk to about my day. Finding the right man was going to be a struggle for me. Unfortunately, Brody moved to Nevada before we developed a relationship. I have had my share of good and bad dates. I think for the most part they were an education for me. I knew Mr. Right was somewhere out there.

Reality Show

MY TWO YOUNGER sisters enjoy watching a lot of reality television shows. One of their favorites is a dating show. Around Christmas in 2009 they surreptitiously signed me up for it. I was completely clueless they entered me. They knew my struggle with dating in Chico, saw me shed a lot of tears with the marine, and wanted me to be with a man who would treat me right. My sisters later explained, "We wanted everyone to see how amazing you are, and you need to step out of your box."

This was all true. I had been living in Chico most of my life and I had a job where I spent most of my time. It was like I was in a little box and somehow a reality show was going to get me out? My life continues to be crazy.

In February of 2010 I received a phone call that little did I know was going to change my life forever.

A TV producer said I had been selected out of many applicants to participate in a dating reality show that coming fall. I was totally confused; I didn't sign up for a dating show, I had never even watched one before. He explained someone had filled out an application for me and sent in photos. I knew right then my two sisters were responsible.

I will never forget this moment. I was at work stand-

ing in the parking lot talking on the phone about the call
with my sisters most of the afternoon. I was somewhat in
a funk. My sisters were ecstatic. They said they knew the
show would call me and that I have to do it. I asked myself
... do what? I didn't even know what the show was about,
or what I "had to do." My sisters told me there is a lot of
fun travel involved and you go on theses amazing dates
with a good-looking man you could possibly fall in love
with. He proposes to one girl that he picks at the very end.
Hmmm ... this kept my interest.

That night I went over to my parents' house and talked with my family about everything. The first thing Dad
asked was, "Do you have to sleep with the guy?" My sisters
cleared that up right away: "No." My parents had never
watched this reality show either, so their questions were as
good as mine. I had *no* clue what I could be getting into.

I decided to call the show and let them know I would
go ahead with the process and see what happens. I figured,
if it's meant to be, it'll happen. I had to admit the timing
could not have been better—I was finished with school,
wasn't in a relationship, and had no plans.

I didn't tell many people because I wanted to wait until
I knew more. I was required to put together a ten-minute
video of myself answering questions so they could see how
I am on camera. Now, the show knew I was a funeral director and embalmer and they, of course, loved that. They
never had an embalmer on their show before. I knew I had
to be careful dealing with that. I did not want anything
to get turned around. My video was about forty minutes
long—apparently I am very comfortable in front of a camera. In fact, I have been doing funeral commercials ever
since I could remember. I may be a little biased, but I have

to say our commercials are pretty good—for funeral commercials. Sorry, I got a little sidetracked there. Let me get back to my story.

My forty-minute video consisted of me talking about how I grew up in the funeral home, and that I am a very normal girl who has not had the best of luck in the dating world. The show loved that kind of stuff, only for me it was all true. No fabrication there (as you have read). I took the camera to the park, and to my apartment, and then we went to a local restaurant. I had a couple good friends in the video talking about what I am like as a friend and answering other questions about me. If I say so myself, it was a pretty good production except it was thirty minutes longer than requested.

I didn't make a copy of the video because I thought if they didn't get the video then it wasn't meant to be; plus I did not know how to copy a DVD—I am technically challenged. Sure enough, they received the video and immediately called saying they loved it (they admitted to fast-forwarding a lot but got the gist of it).

The office asked if I could come to a weekend casting call out of town so they could meet me in person and do some on-camera interviews. The appointment was on a weekend I did not have to work and I had no plans. See a pattern here and how everything has been working out way too easily? Crazy scary.

I flew south and met with many producers doing on-camera interviews. I was comfortable with everyone and actually enjoyed talking in front of the camera. I am an open girl as it is (my mom says sometimes I am too open), so being in front of a camera was natural to me.

After talking with some of the producers and learning

more about the show and what I was really getting myself into, I became at ease with everything and was getting ready to commit to the show. I learned I would basically be competing to win a man's heart. I was not going to be the only girl there. Not only that, we wouldn't know anything about the man I was about to try falling in love with. I guess you could say it was going to be like a blind date, except many other girls would be eyeing the same guy.

I even met with a therapist, which was required for all those selected for the show. She had to ask questions about my life. I never had a session with a therapist before, but I really enjoyed meeting with her and understand why many people see one.

I was okay with all of this, I was not bothered with the fact it was somewhat a competition. I was ready for a challenge—I was ready to fall in love. I had only told two guys in my life I loved them (soccer boyfriend and the marine). I was excited to hopefully fall in love with a *man*—a man who did not need any rescuing. I was hoping the man I was about to meet was going to be okay with my job. Yikes.

I came home after the casting weekend and shared my experience at a family meeting (these are regular with us). I told them I felt very comfortable throughout the entire weekend, in front of the camera, with the producers, the fact that I won't know anything about man I am going to meet, and of course being okay with everyone watching television knowing I am a funeral director.

The decision was made; I wanted to do this. I was ready for a change in my life. I was twenty-five and been working hard at the funeral home for five years. I was excited to not only have the possibility of falling in love and being vulnerable, but to have the chance of a lifetime.

My immediate family was obviously on board with me going and were excited for me. My close friends were also supportive and offered their closets for me to raid before leaving. I totally took them up on their offers—it's amazing how much stuff I was able to jam into three suitcases.

Speaking of clothes, I have a hilarious story about picking out one of my outfits for the trip. My first shopping trip was to Chico Mall, and I have to say, our mall is not what you'd call upscale. It's small with limited options, except for the great Forever 21 (as you can imagine, all us girls wear the same clothes).

I had to find the perfect dress for my first night meeting this man. I walked up and down the mall without luck. I even ordered a dress online, which can be risky, for about three hundred dollars. I received the dress a week before I was leaving for the show. It didn't fit—it looked horrible! It was a red dress, which is a good color on me, but it looked like I was swimming in it. Mom was in the room when I tried it on. I was freaking out!

I don't have any more time, I was thinking. What am I going to do? Mom said she'd like to take me to Sears and help look for a gown. I thought … Sears? You have to be joking. "*Mom,* you buy appliances at Sears, not clothes." She said she had a Sears credit card and that moms know best. Forcing myself, we headed over to Sears.

Sure enough, the first dress that caught my eye was this beautiful canary yellow gown. Mom looked at me with those "I told you so" eyes. I tried on the gown. Perfect fit! Want to know the best part? It was only twenty dollars. I guess you can say my yellow canary dress kicked my sweet red three-hundred-dollar dress out the door. Mothers do know best.

After my suitcases were packed and I was taking care of last minute details, it was time to let the employees at the funeral home know I was going to be on this reality show and would be gone for quite some time. I wasn't exactly sure when I would be back. Most of the employees were supportive, but some were concerned I'd get emotionally hurt.

Mom and Dad fully supported my decision. The employees realized this. All agreed I could take time off work to take advantage of this once-in-a-lifetime opportunity. Now that work was taken care of, I was ready to take a *giant* leap of faith.

The night I left, our family had a huge barbecue as a nice way to say goodbye before I headed into this crazy adventure. Comforted by my family's support of the decision and a group prayer, I knew this was meant to be, and I had peace with that.

As I loaded my luggage I discovered an attached note, "I love you. —Dad." I told myself not to cry, but it didn't work. My mom took me to the airport and she, like most mothers would, cried and did not want to send me off. I told her I was going to be okay and not to worry. I should have known you can't say that to your mother—she's going to worry *no* matter what. I kissed her goodbye and promised I would see her soon.

Fall was in the air. I was off to the unknown and excited about it. I knew my phone would be confiscated—an adjustment that could cause anxiety. I've never gone anywhere without it. I wouldn't be allowed contact with the outside world, which I accepted as a growing experience.

I was greeted by one of the producers of the show. She showed me my hotel room and took my phone. This is hard to admit, but after she left the room, I started crying. I somewhat felt like I was away in prison camp. I opened my suitcase and saw a note inside. It was from my mom: "I will be thinking about you every day. I love you, Mom." That did not help with my crying.

I regained my composure and assured myself I was going to have a good time and enjoy every moment.

That night I put on my Sears dress. I was ready to meet this man whom I was possibly going to fall in love with. Since I hadn't seen this reality show before, I only had vague ideas how everything worked. All I knew was I would be stepping out of a limo in a couple hours and must be prepared to introduce myself.

I did just that. I stepped out of the limo, took a deep breath (of course he noticed my huge inhale), and I slowly walked over to him. I say slowly, because I was *so* concerned I was going to slip. I wasn't too nervous about him, or that there were about twenty cameras next to me, but the walkway was slippery. And I tend to fall, sleep, rip, and do about anything relating to the word falling.

Success! … I did not slip and fall. I introduced myself to this man and the first thing he said was, "I love your dress." Ohhhh if he only knew the story behind the Sears dress. After our brief introduction I was led inside the mansion to a living room full of beautiful women. Suddenly, my confidence level dropped. I felt like I wanted to turn right around and go home (despite the fact I just introduced myself to a beautiful tall man).

I introduced myself to the other women and counted twenty-nine. How the heck am I going to win this man's heart with twenty-nine other women trying the same thing? What on Earth did my sisters get me into?

Let me say, I am a confident independent woman, and I am really good in difficult situations. I have my experience as a funeral director to thank for that. I needed to get myself to realize that if I can meet with bereaved families every day, I can handle these other women and the journey to falling in love.

That first night was rough—not just for me, but for all the women. We all wanted to spend time with Stephen. All the girls had a moment to spend with Stephen and some even interrupted others to get more attention and time. I was *not* one of those. I did not want to have to chase him around. Little did I know, I would have to up my game to get more time.

The way the show worked, a woman would be sent home each day until there was one. At the end of the first night we all gathered to find out if we are going to stay another night and get to know Stephen more. Steven gave each woman a red rose. There weren't enough roses for everyone. Anyone who didn't get a rose went home. I was hoping to be staying because I just packed a butt load of clothes and this better be worth it. I stayed.

With twenty girls left, we moved into the mansion and shared rooms with each other. Great, this is going to be like a military camp, but instead of guns, it's curling irons—yikes!

Stephen would choose a girl he wanted to take out on a date; it could be a group date, or an individual date. We all wanted individual dates with Stephen because it gave us more time with him to get familiar. I ended up going on the first group date to a beautiful poolside suite, along with sixteen other girls. No way in heck was I going to get to know this guy on a date with sixteen others. I was careful with what I said and my actions—everything was being filmed. I was never too concerned about the cameras because I was not a crazy girl (I can't say that for everyone there).

I did not get a lot of time with Stephen that day, but felt confident he was not going to send me home without more time. Throughout that first week, I watched a couple other girls go on individual dates with Stephen. They would come back with strong feelings for him. My feelings about him were not very strong because I hardly knew him.

At the end of the week Stephen had to send a couple more girls home, allowing the rest of us to move onto the next week full of dates. Safe again, along with seventeen others remaining.

I did not get an individual date but another group date. This time it was with only ten more girls. Getting better here. The group date consisted of us making a trailer for a movie. We had to compete for the lead roll. The girl who got the lead roll would be able to spend more time with Stephen. We girls had to show our kickboxing moves to Stephen and a trainer who was there to teach us how to do awesome maneuvers like you see Angelina Jolie do in one of her movies. It just so happens I love kickboxing and take a class on a regular basis back home. I ended up getting the lead roll in the trailer.

I spent a lot of time with Stephen. We even played a role in the trailer where I had to kiss him. I say the word "had" because I really didn't want to kiss him in front of the jealous girls. Well, that was shot out the window. In the last scene of the trailer, Stephen and I did our kissing scene while the other ten girls stood offstage watching us. Talk about awkward! I don't even want to mention my grandmother having to watch this part when the show aired. That could be a chapter in itself.

Okay, back to the awkwardness of the group date. After Stephen and I completed the last scene, we all went to a poolside dinner and watched the movie trailer. I have to admit, we did a pretty good job! My feelings for Stephen began that night. No, not just because we kissed (a couple times) but because we were finally able to get some time together and I was enjoying our conversations. He was a gentleman.

At the end of that week Stephen had to send more girls home but I knew I was safe. The hard part of all this was being unable to call up my sisters or friends and tell them about Stephen. That was not easy getting used to. During dates and the days we were getting to know Stephen, we would do interviews on camera about how we are feeling and our journey. I used that time like it was my journal. I would talk about how I was starting to fall for Stephen and I wanted to get to know him more.

I bet you are wondering about the drama within the mansion. Well as you can imagine, if you put twenty girls anywhere together and add one man to the mix, there are going to be some catfights, claws, and tears. Growing up, I was hardly ever involved with drama in school or the workplace, I kept that out of my life; I was good at avoiding drama. I also kept it out of the show for the most part. I did not get in the middle of the catfights. In fact, I ended up being a mediator at times. Many of the girls were able to talk with me, on or off camera, about difficult times they had, usually concerning death. All the girls knew I was a funeral director and they felt comfortable with me. In the beginning I was spending more time with them than I was with Stephen.

I have to say, though, being with the ladies wasn't always perfect. I had some hard times with the competition part of the show. I was not used to competition, especially over a man. All the girls I was staying with in the mansion were after the same guy I was developing feelings for. This situation seemed so abnormal. It's hard for me to explain to you how I felt knowing the girls did not really want me there—we all felt the same way about each other—we all wanted Stephen to ourselves.

Have you read *How to be a Hepburn in a Hilton World* by Jordan Christy? If you haven't, and you're a woman, put it on your reading list. The author breaks it down for us: it's not that hard to remain classy in a world like this. She rallies women to pursue knowledge, dignity, and class. Some say TV reality stars do the opposite of her guidelines and refer to female reality TV stars as "Stupid Girls." I learned there's a reason behind "reality" shows beyond the stereotype. Our show was not scripted fiction—it was unpredictable *drama!*

The twenty-nine girls I started with were a mix of (Paris) Hiltons and (Audrey and Katherine) Hepburns. The diversity created drama. I was dealing with some Hiltons during the show and wanted to make sure I remained a Hepburn and not become a part of the Stupid Girls!

It wasn't always easy; some girls had group or individual conversations about each other. For example, I would overhear or be a part of a conversation talking about what we thought Stephen was doing on his date with another girl; or how we didn't think a particular girl would be a good match for him. I tried to keep out of certain conversations that I could later regret. I listened a lot. I was assertive when needed and didn't allow other girls to cross the line with me. I was careful.

Now, I've said the girls knew I was a funeral director and embalmer. Well, funny thing, Stephen did *not* know this yet. I had managed to avoid bringing up the "family business." It wasn't difficult because I didn't share a lot of time with him yet. I wasn't too excited to tell him about my job. You recall how my dates have turned out after they found out I'm a funeral director.

We were down to eleven girls in the mansion—and told we were going to Las Vegas! I had never been there. It's true; I had never been to Vegas. But once you hear what I did, you'll agree it was worth the wait.

I got my first individual date with Stephen. He invited me to go on a shopping spree! I asked him to tell me a second time because I didn't believe him the first. This is like every girl's dream to go on a shopping spree—especially in a city like Las Vegas. We shopped in one of the nicest malls in the world. We went from store to store trying on different clothes and having a blast. Remember, I come from Chico so my shopping experience has been limited all my life, which made this was spree crazy awesome! There were some names I had never heard of (I pretended I did, though).

Lastly, Stephen took me into Fendi and I was in heaven. He told me to pick out an outfit for dinner, including a pair of shoes. Holy *cow*! This was too good to be true. I picked out a beautiful gray dress and a fabulous pair of Fendi shoes. After shopping, I joined the other girls in our suite. I wasn't looking forward to showing them what I got. *But,* I did. I think their faces turned green with envy.

I changed into my Fendi dress and shoes. Stephen arrived at our suite to pick me up for our dinner date. He was handsomely dressed up. I was nervous because I knew I needed to tell him about being a funeral director and had no idea how he was going to react. Worst-case scenario, he sends me home that night and I at least get some really cute shoes out of it. All the women watched us leave, and I knew they were going to have some unfriendly things to say while I was gone.

We dined on top of the mall with a wide view overlooking Las Vegas. It was beautiful. Neon lights from the casinos were aglow. During dinner I told Stephen, "There's something you should know about me ..." He said he was excited to get to know me.

I revealed I am a funeral director and embalmer. Pause for reaction. Stephen looked at me and asked, I kid you not, "What do you have to do to embalm someone?" I was taken aback. I did not see that question coming, especially the first question. I took a sip of wine and asked him if he really wanted to know, because I was willing to talk about the process of embalming over dinner, but I didn't know if he really was interested, or just being polite. He assured me he wanted to know. So over our sushi dinner I told Stephen about the process. Like I said, I am able to talk about embalming over dinner, it does not bother me. Stephen kept asking me questions about the process and I continued to answer him. Stephen began to adjust his collar but still asked me questions. He said this was the most interesting date he has ever been on. I don't doubt that.

Once Stephen got the 411 on embalming, I started asking about his life; what his interests are. He owned a business and lived in Texas. He asked questions about my family. I also told him about my sweet cross-eyed cat, Peaches. All in all we had a great time at dinner. I could easily see myself with Stephen. He gave me a rose that night and sent another woman home. I was able to stay another week. We were down to nine girls.

As the girls were being sent home, it was becoming harder to say goodbye. We had been together for weeks and were forming friendships. It was sad seeing them go but at the same time it was a good because the less girls, the better. Bittersweet.

The remaining girls and I were told our next adventure was going to take place in Costa Rica with Stephen and we needed to pack up and get our passports ready. I had never been out of the country before, and I was so excited. My feelings for Stephen were growing. I was having an eye-opening experience with all the travel and new feelings developing for the bachelor. We were off to Costa Rica.

In Costa Rica I ended up in another group date. Stephen took us deep into the Costa Rica jungle to rappel down a one hundred-seventy-foot waterfall. I am not the kind of girl who is comfortable with heights. I tend to freak out! Well, I volunteered first. I knew if I didn't go first I would never go because I'd be too scared. Annnnd, I admit, I was trying to show off in front of Stephen so he knew I was adventurous. A woman's gotta do what a woman's gotta do!

After the week in Costa Rica I made it pretty clear to the camera that I was falling for Stephen, my feelings were growing, and I wanted him to meet my family in Chico. I was hoping I would have the opportunity to bring him home.

Our next destination was the island of Anguilla (Caribbean). I think I was more excited to have another stamp on my passport than anything. There were now only six of us women left. It was hard to believe we started out with thirty and now I was one of six. I received an individual date in Anguilla. Stephen and I rode bikes around the island and stopped at a local farmers market where we had yummy local food, drinks, and played dominos. It was the best date I ever had. It was so my kind of date. In Chico we have a lot of farmers markets and I always ride my bike through Bidwell Park. So this date was right up my alley.

I ended up telling Stephen I was beginning to fall in love with him. You may be thinking, how can you fall in love on a reality television show? Stephen made it pretty easy to fall for him. He was from the South, had wonderful manners, didn't mind my job, and made me feel like a woman. I really never had that. I was used to rescuing the guys I dated. Stephen did not need any rescuing and I was very attracted to that.

The position Stephen was in would have been hard for any man. You have many beautiful women competing for your attention and you have to try and make every woman feel special. I learned to focus on what he and I had, and not what he had with the other girls. I noticed the girls who focused on everyone else's but not their own relationship, messed up. They struggled and were sent home fast. I was confident in what I had with Stephen.

The week in Anguilla was one of the hardest weeks for myself and the remaining five girls. We were all at the point where we had developed feelings for Stephen and had nothing else we wanted to share with each other. No one wanted to hear about how much we were falling for him. We kept really quiet that week. Since we had spent a lot of time together, I became close to another girl who was still on the show. We kept a friendly distance, though, because we were both vying for the same guy. We knew that no matter what happened, we would remain friends after the show.

On the last day in Anguilla, we found out two more girls were going home and the remaining four would bring Stephen back to our hometowns. I became one of the top four.

The four of us were separated at this point, which we were happy about because we had nothing more we wanted to share with each other. It was becoming way too difficult to talk about our feelings.

Once we arrived in the states I gathered my thoughts about everything. I was getting anxious to see my family. It was around seven weeks since I spoke to anyone I truly loved. I knew the feelings I had for Stephen were real—they weren't influenced by anyone but myself. It was all me and I could not wait until Stephen met my family.

I thought if Stephen and I were meant to be together then he would choose me with the final rose and everything would all work out. I wanted Stephen to see my place of work before we went any further. I knew, from our Las Vegas date, he was interested in the embalming process, but I wanted to be sure he was comfortable enough to marry someone who's a funeral director and embalmer.

Stephen met me at the funeral home that morning for an exclusive tour. I know, I know, I know, what was I thinking? Well, I was thinking that the situation we were already in was hard enough. I had been on this soul-searching journey to fall in love. I was vulnerable, tired, scared and excited all at the same time. This was all out of my comfort zone. I thought I needed to know now if Stephen was okay with my family and profession before we or I got too deeply involved. Let the tour begin.

I took Stephen into the mausoleum and showed him the different crypts and niches. I explained a mausoleum is like an indoor cemetery that's all above ground. The crypts are for caskets and the niches are for cremated remains. I could see Stephen was a little uncomfortable in the mausoleum so I told him he should think of it as a place full of love; not death. There are hundreds of family members entombed: husband and wives, children, aunts and uncles. From then on Stephen felt better.

Next we went into the prep room where I showed him the different instruments used for embalming. Stephen had asked me all those questions about embalming, so I thought he would be more interested with the prep room. And he was. Throughout the tour I was feeling pretty confident that he was doing okay and would be able to handle everything. I want to add, I don't normally take my dates to the funeral home for romance. Trust me, I already have a hard enough time talking to a guy about it. You may be wondering why I took Stephen to the funeral home and not other men. Like I said before, considering the situation we were in, I felt it was the right thing to do. If he was going to be proposing to me within that next two weeks, I wanted him to have a true understanding of how I grew up. Plus, I wanted him to have a different perspective on death.

Now that Stephen had the full tour of Newton-Bracewell Chico Funeral Home, I was ready to have him meet my family. Before leaving, Stephen sat me down and said he really did learn a lot about the process of death, and now feels more comfortable with it. He told me his grandfather had died many years ago and he was not able to handle everything well. Stephen said he wished he had a funeral director who was as caring as I. His words meant a lot to me.

Stephen and I headed over to my parents' house. I wasn't nervous about this part of our day whatsoever. I knew my family was going to love Stephen and would be happy for me no matter what. I don't know if I mentioned this yet, but Stephen was from another state and he made it pretty clear he wanted whomever he married to move to his hometown. This had been a struggle for me throughout the entire journey. I never voiced my concern to Stephen because I am a huge believer that when you are in love, you do things you never thought you would do. I didn't want to be closed-minded. I knew his need was going to be hard to explain to my family.

My whole family was crying when we arrived (remember, the camera was always present where we went). For the first time in nearly seven weeks, I could hug them. Once introductions were over we sat down and, with Stephen next to me, I announced I was falling in love and recounted the adventures Stephen and I had been sharing for several weeks. My sisters could tell I was actually falling in love with the Southern gentleman. In all truth, I was.

I had the chance to talk with my mom (on camera) and of course she was just happy her daughter was back home. I told her that if things worked out with Stephen and me, I would most likely be moving to his home state. She was a little concerned about that (like any parent would). My family had a hard time grasping I was in love with Stephen because everything was happening so fast. Stephen talked with my sisters who are really protective. They told him they were the ones who put me up to everything. They had seen other shows and were happy he was the one I was falling in love with. They approved.

Then came time for me to talk with my dad. This was not

Newton family: Vanessa, Ric, Shawntel, Colene, Destiny

as easy for me. My dad was very deliberate and not afraid to voice his opinion. We spoke in private (with cameras of course). He said he was a little hesitant with the thought of me moving away from Chico to be with Stephen. He also said the Chico community would miss me a great deal. I knew this. I knew that if I ever left Chico things would be hard because I'd leave my job, friends, and family. I have lived in Chico all my life and I have served many families at the funeral home. I told Dad that if Stephen and I are both in love, "things will work out the way they should."

While I was gone, Dad said, a friend of mine had died in a horrible car accident. The day of the accident my friend's mother came into the funeral home wanting to meet with me, and only me. Since I was gone, my dad stepped in, met with my friend's mother and father, and made the arrangements. It was really hard for the mother; she wanted me to be there for her. Some think Dad should not have told me about the death of my friend, but I am not sorry he did. He wanted me to know I was missed and I have made a huge impact on the Chico community.

It came time for my dad to talk with Stephen privately. "I know my daughter, and I know she is falling in love with you," he told Stephen. Stephen was unable to say much about his feelings because he had to be fair to all four of us remaining girls, whose families he was meeting each show. He told Dad he had strong feelings for me and I have a lot of qualities he wants in a wife.

After dinner and the serious discussions with my family, it was time for Stephen to leave. I told him my feelings had not changed, I was in love with him, and it felt good to be in love with a man. Before I walked Stephen out, Dad spoke on behalf of my family, "Shawntel ... Stephen, if you both are meant to be together, than everything will work out the way it's suppose to and we support you in whatever you do. And we love you." That meant a lot to me and to Stephen. My dad gave his blessing.

I said goodbye to Stephen, then said goodbye to my family and was off to New York without him. Stephen was scheduled to meet the other three girls' families and I had to force myself not to think about it and focus on what he and I had.

At the end of the week I was in New York City waiting to find out if Stephen was going to send me home or keep me on the journey of love with him. I put on a beautiful dress and said hello to the other three girls. We waited in a beautiful suite to hear his decision. I felt pretty confident Stephen was going to keep me. I thought everything went well with my family, and with the funeral home. Stephen made his decision: he gave each of the other three girls a rose. I was sent home!

I said goodbye on camera to the three remaining girls (one of whom is now a best friend). Then Stephen walked me out to a limo. He told me he really had a nice time with my family and how amazing I was, blah blah. I was in complete shock. I did not see that happening. I had just opened up to him and told him that I was in love and even willing to move from my hometown to be with him. Boy did that backfire.

Stephen dismissed me in the nicest way possible, but I could have cared less at that moment. I was just confused and felt so alone. I didn't need any sugarcoating; I just wanted to go home.

I did my closing interview in the limo and was very honest about how I was in love with Stephen—he was an amazing man who was easy to fall in love with. I was not used to being in love with a man, nor was I used to feeling so special. The last guy I said I love you to was the marine and I did not feel like a woman in that relationship. I flew home the next morning, my phone was returned by the producer who escorted me to the airport, and I was pushed back into my reality in Chico. Weird.

My Grief

I WAS GONE a total of seven and a-half weeks traveling, sharing my feelings in front of a camera, falling in love, and just being completely out of my comfort zone. Once I arrived in Chico I was in a funk. I was still confused with everything and unfortunately was unable to talk with Stephen about my confusion. In a normal breakup you can talk to each other about what happened, and have more of a closure with everything. In my strange, abnormal situation, I was not able or allowed to talk to him about anything. I was cut off for now. The only thing I knew was he was not in love with me and was going to be engaged to one of the other three girls within two weeks.

I came home on a Friday. That night I went out to dinner with my parents and sisters and told them about everything that happened since they saw me at home with Stephen. They were a little shocked themselves. They did not think I would be coming home right after our hometown date. My family did tell me, though; they did not believe he was the guy for me (family sometimes just knows). My family was happy I was home and not engaged to a man whom I was not meant to be with. They saw I was hurt; they knew things were going to be tough for a while.

I went to work Monday morning. Not a good idea. I met with a family but was unable to give them my full attention during their grief. I knew this was not fair to them, or to me. I, too, was grieving. How could I serve a family during their difficult time, while I was going through similar stages of grief? I couldn't talk about my adventure or grief to anyone (except my family) because the show was not due to air until the next year. For a couple months I had to remain in silence before even my friends could know what happened. I did not go to work on Tuesday, instead I cried in my bed and told my parents I needed to take at least a week off work and catch my breath. They understood.

That week I became very ill. My immune system had shut down for a bit—my body was fatigued. I had been traveling for so long and my immune system was so built up, that once I came home I got sick. I slept for most of the week and talked/vented to my sisters a lot. I would become angry at times and frustrated with how everything ended. I did not want to socialize with any of my friends for a while; I was just too tired.

The word was all around town that I went on a reality show; I had been gone for a long time. I knew the secret would leak eventually.

After the week of my seclusion from the world, I stepped back into the workplace feeling better. Remember how I was talking about consulting with a therapist during my casting weekend? Well, she came in handy during my time of grief. Since I was only allowed to talk to my immediate family about all the emotions I was dealing with, it was so nice to have a connection with someone who knew what I had been through. She helped me understand these emotions were normal and I was being healthy about my grieving. Talking with my therapist made me realize that when I am serving families within the funeral home, I am a lot like a therapist to those who are grieving. Usually with a sudden/accidental death we, as funeral directors, encourage family members to get involved with a support group or meet with a counselor for aftercare. I so badly wanted a support group while I was dealing with my grief but was unable to because I was forbidden to talk to anyone about my experiences until the show aired.

I talked with my therapist on a weekly basis and she would call to ask how I was doing. It was a huge relief to talk with her and share things I was not allowed to talk about with my friends.

Weeks passed—I was very much on a healthy streak of being out of love with Stephen. Knowing Stephen simply wasn't in love with me helped me fall out of love with him, which made things easier for me. I had no regrets with how I was on the show; I knew I remained myself the entire time.

Before the show even aired, while I was recovering from grief, I heard the first negative rumor starting to spread about me—a moment I'll never forget. My therapist warned me about the blogs and Internet. I had never thought about it. I was so wrapped up in falling out of love with Stephen that, thankfully, I was not reading or hearing the rumors. I was not used to people being mean to me, or saying ugly things about me. I received a hurtful email at work from some stranger. It upset me. My first reaction was to reply, defending myself. However, I wisely did *not* give the stranger a reaction. This was just the beginning. Let the rumors fly.

THE HOLIDAYS WERE already upon us. Previews of the reality show were beginning to air. I was no longer in love with Stephen, I could grieve and catch up on my sleep, and my social life was back on track (oh, and I caught up on all the emails and messages that accumulated during my seven-week disappearance). The website was up and running for the prerecorded reality show. A friend called. My picture and short bio were posted along with the other twenty-nine girls'. I raced home to check the website and see how my photo turned out. I was honestly excited for the show to start so my friends could watch all the fun adventures I experienced. Browsing the show's website, I noticed a tab for blogs. This is what my therapist warned me against reading. But it was like the tab was asking me to click it. I was curious what the public were saying about me. From that point on, my skin began thickening.

Even though the show had not begun, the public was already passing judgment on us. Someone said, "Her job is just too creepy. I absolutely bet she does not end up with him." Another wrote, "Eww she is a funeral director, she needs to go home and get back to working with the dead." This is just a taste of what I read the first day the website was up. And, like I said, the show had not even started yet. Since my bio said I was a funeral director, people were already judging me harshly. I will quote more bloggers later.

I was a little upset and called my sisters … okay wait, let me rephrase that: I called my sisters and I was *very mad!* I could not believe the judgment I was reading solely based on my small bio and a photo. My sister advised me to "get off the computer, step away from the computer." Those were sagacious words—I complied. Not reading the blogs was the only way to avoid being hurt. Well, I must admit, following her advice only lasted a week or so.

It was almost like a habit for me: I would go into work, immediately log onto my computer, read the blogs, my feelings would get really hurt, and I would have a horrible day. Earlier in this book I recounted the writings on the walls in high school, and how some (mostly girls) were talking about me in school and I came home crying. Well, it was like that but times a thousand. My mom had told me to remember, "Stop allowing others to define who you are." Mom was right, but it was still very hard to ignore the things being said about me.

A friend of mine has been dealing with being in the public eye for many years. I knew he'd be the best person to call for support. He could relate to me reading the blogs and Googleing myself. He told me of the times he started replying to some of the bloggers and defending himself. I felt much better knowing this was normal and I was not the only one with the problem. He said the only way to get away from the bad press is to not go looking for it. Don't visit the bloggers' websites, and keep thick skin. Not too thick, but enough to be able to handle it. After conversing with him, my skin thickened and I avoided the blogs! This was good discipline for me because the show had not started. I was preparing for it to be broadcast and knew the good/bad press would soon start its commentary. Bring it on!

Once the holidays were over I was ready for the show to start and to see the end results of Stephen's journey to love. I had my hunch as to whom he'd end up picking. Finally, my friends could find out what I had been doing. I was looking forward to discussing the show with them.

One of my good friends who lives in Oregon visited her

parents' home in Chico for the premier airing of the show. Her mother wanted to throw a big potluck party for thirty of my family and friends. I was so excited. My friends made Team Shawntel t-shirts for everyone. Each friend handed me a rose as she came into the house. My parents made a toast and we started watching the first episode. As the show went on, I started to feel a little funny. Memories began to creep up. I just felt a little overwhelmed. It was okay, though. This time I had my family and close friends with me and I was loved.

The next day, my entire life changed. All of Chico heard about me being on the show, I was receiving calls from magazines (which my contract prohibited me from talking to), and I started to get letters and emails from that day on. For the most part, everything was positive. Chico was thrilled to have a local on a national television show. I did not visit the websites; I was good at avoiding the blogs,

Friends wearing Team Shawntel t-shirts gather to watch TV reality show

which could have turned this journey into a negative experience.

The weeks went by—the more who watched me on TV, the more I was recognized in stores. People wanted to talk to me about the show and take their pictures with me. This was all so new. Strangers had never wanted their take pictures taken with me. I was even signing autographs. Mothers approached me—they loved it that their daughter could watch a classy, professional woman on the show; someone to look up to. Those words meant so much to me.

I didn't realize how many people watched this reality show—the funeral profession drew a lot of positive exposure. Every time I did an interview on camera, my name would be on screen along with "Funeral Director." That was satisfying to see. I know my professors at mortuary school were impressed!

I was enjoying the process; I tried to turn everything into a positive outlook no matter what. As I watched episodes of the show, sometimes I would see one of the girls saying something that was not so nice about me. I learned not to let it bother me. I remained classy and had no regrets. People around town sometimes asked if I would do it again, or if I regretted the experience? I would always say, "No regrets and I am glad I took the risk."

Each week we friends got together at one of our houses to watch the show. During commercials we talked about the details and more of the drama. Towards the eighth week it was time for my last episode. Some of my friends had no idea—there was going to be a lot of surprise that night. My parents joined us because they of course knew it was the night I was sent home and they wanted to provide support in case I needed it.

My friends saw our family on television and watched Dad express his concerns to Stephen and me on our hometown date. They got a kick out of the tour I gave Stephen of the funeral home because they, too, have been to my workplace and know a lot about it from my conversations. After some giggles from watching Stephen with my family, tears started. My friends and family saw me cry as I watched myself get sent home after my hometown date. They cried with me. It was strange watching myself crying on a recorded television show while simultaneously crying live in the living room. My feelings for Stephen did not surface, but I just felt sad after that episode. I relived my journey and it was exciting. But it was also difficult to revisit.

I was just bragging to you how I was doing so well avoiding blogs or going on the Internet and reading the hurtful rumors and comments. Well, I have to admit another weakness that happened after the airing of my hometown date. ...

I went onto the show's website that night to read what people were saying about me, I knew there was going to be a lot of fuss about the funeral home. I knew there would be many who would say I was wrong to give him a tour. A question on the blog asked, "Would you marry a mortician?" Of course I immediately clicked on it to read what they were saying. Here're some examples: "NO WAY jose, I just couldn't be around all that day in and day out. Shawntel is not only a mortician but a funeral director and that would be tough stuff." "I think the reason he sent her home had more to do with her taking over the family business ... that would mean she would have to move ... she looked like she wanted to be rescued from taking over her dad's business." "I feel like her dad was being a jerk. Like you gotta carry on this death business. I don't like him." "I loved Shawntel, I just think the job would indeed be a hurdle for many people. I feel bad for Shawntel, but I think Shawntel's profession and family pressure spelled the end for her chances." "I give Shawntel credit, she really stood up to her dad, without showing him any disrespect, she held her ground." "Shawntel should marry a pathologist or firefighter."

It was really hard to read posts about my family and how some thought it was forcing me into the profession of funeral services. All my life, Mom and Dad have been supportive and just want us girls to be happy.

Some of the posts were not easy to read, and I kept asking myself why was I even taking the time to read them? But I could not help it. I cried a little and allowed myself to grieve for a moment (okay, longer than a moment, like a week or so).

After I was sent home on the eighth episode, my email went crazy. People from all over the nation were contacting me. I went into work the next day and had hundreds of emails from fans, funeral directors, mothers, fathers, and even grandparents waiting in my inbox. They were mostly encouraging emails that made me feel good. A lot of mothers emailed me that I deserve someone better than Stephen, and that I shined a new light onto death.

Millions of people watched Stephen tour a funeral home and millions were able to see the inside of a mausoleum, prep room, crematory, and an arrangement office. I know many people who have never been to a funeral in their life, let alone a prep room or crematory area. For the audience, the exposure to our industry was surely unique—for me, shining a light on the funeral industry began opening doors of opportunity. …

New Opportunities

THE SHOW WAS over. Stephen chose a beautiful woman I had gotten to know, to receive the final rose. It was the woman I thought he would choose. I wished them nothing but happiness. Now it was on to my own happiness.

Working at the funeral home was a little different following the show's final episode. I never had so much public exposure (aside from local commercials I did for the funeral home, which were mostly elderly people squeezing my cheek in the grocery store). The nationwide exposure would lead to excitement and opportunities. I was ready.

Not only was I receiving emails and letters, but I was also getting flowers and balloons via the funeral home. It was nice having flowers sent to me and not for a funeral service. I don't think I'll ever stop recalling my mom ask Dad on their anniversary, "Are these flowers really from you, or are they from a funeral service?" The gifts were from kind people (boys sent the flowers) who felt badly about me being sent home. I even received phone numbers from people all across the states.

Daily, my inbox was filled with letters from fans who wanted me to know how much of an impact I made on them and how death is not as scary as they once believed.

One of the first letters was from a woman who told me her grandfather died a couple years ago and she was unable to attend their funeral. "Somehow seeing the mausoleum on TV," she wrote, "brought a bit of closure to me for not being able to be there. I felt compelled to write to you and let you know how much I appreciated hearing your thoughtful perspective and attitude on life and death. ... Here is one thing you said on the show that will always stay with me. ... You said that it was always sad ... that there are many happy moments too and most importantly, you said, there is so much love in here." Her letter made my eyes fill with tears—only this time they were tears of appreciation. She helped me remember exactly why I love helping families and, hopefully, the impact I had on many people who watched the show.

I opened a handwritten letter from a twelve-year-old girl saying, "I am your biggest fan, I think your job is so cool. When I grow up I want to be a funeral director just like *you*." I was so tickled by the letter. Never in my life would I have imagined making an impact on a young girl who thinks my job is cool and can't wait to do the same thing when she grows up. I saved her letter and wrote back telling her to follow her dreams.

Now, not all my emails were positive, but at this point in my life after learning how to cope with the negativity, I could read the emails without allowing them to hurt me as they did in the past. Even some funeral directors emailed to say I was wrong to allow Stephen into the prep room. I will say now, I do not think there was anything wrong with the way I handled the tour or the way I talked to Stephen about death. I discarded those emails.

As I was telling you, Chico enjoyed the exposure as well.

Different organizations asked me to come and share my experience on a personal level and to talk about what it was like growing up in the funeral home. This was so exciting for me. I love speaking in front of people anyway, so I was all for it.

I spoke at every Rotary, Lions, Exchange and retirement club in Chico. My spirits lifted when I talked not only about my fun experience on the show, but how I was just able to handle myself with grace and integrity. I had been speaking to groups before then. After I graduated from mortuary school, a favorite professor asked me to speak to her class about death and dying, along with what it was like growing up in the funeral industry. I have been speaking to her students every semester till this day.

Word was getting around town that I was doing a lot of speaking engagements and the feedback I received was very encouraging. I learned I had a gift of not only care-giving but public speaking. I enjoyed it so much I always looked forward to my next speaking engagement. One of the pastors from our church asked me to speak to his youth group about dating and the pressures students face today. Honestly, my first thought was … what the heck do I know about dating? All my relationships had mostly failed *and,* to top if off, I was just dumped on national television. Ha! Well, despite my failed relationships and a public breakup, I was on board with speaking to the students about dating and knowing how to handle certain pressures.

I didn't realize the impact I made on them until many approached me afterwards with more questions about life and even about death. I was thankful that day for my failed relationships and my profession.

There would be days when tourists driving through our

small city dropped by work to meet "the funeral girl" from that show. Their visits were unexpectedly fun. On a serious note, many families have requested to meet with me as their funeral director because they watched me on the show and felt as if they knew me really well and were comfortable with me. I have been honored to help.

You may have Facebook, Twitter, LinkedIn or some sort of website—well I am guilty of Facebook and Twitter. There are many advantages of having an Internet presence. For example, a woman looking for me after watching the show found my Facebook page. Her husband was dying of cancer and she wanted me to meet with her and her daughters when the time came. She lives in a smaller town outside of Chico. There are other good local funeral homes that could have helped with her husband's services, but she searched the Web until she found me.

Regrettably, a week after we had exchanged emails, her husband died at home. I met with her and her two beautiful daughters. We all went over arrangements. Sometimes it is hard to separate myself from the families I've served. I connected with this family on a personal level with no regrets about remaining close. In fact, we frequently get together for dinner. Thankfully, they found me on Facebook.

I MENTIONED BEFORE that the funeral profession was delighted about the exposure the reality show brought to the industry. Well, I was asked to speak at our annual California Funeral Director Association (yes, the same association I received my scholarship from in San Jose) convention—all expenses paid. I could bring a guest, so I invited my old roommate from college to ride with me to Monterey. This was a big deal for me. I was thrilled! I had never

Shawntel addresses the CFDA convention in Monterey

been asked to speak at a convention. I felt honored to be part of a convention I remember attending as a child with my dad who is past president.

My parents were glad but not surprised. Mom proudly loves to watch me speak. The presentation would be recorded for her—she was too swamped at work to attend.

At the social mixer, I saw my professors from mortuary college and became acquainted with more funeral directors, like I did when I received my scholarship from CFDA. I wondered if anyone was really going to attend my presentation in the early morning or even cared I was on some reality show.

I was the first speaker. The entire room was filled with directors, students, spouses, and even guests of the hotel who heard I was going to be speaking. I felt so special and could not believe the impact I brought on these people. The title of my presentation was, "Funeral Directors Need Love Too." Hmmm that would be a good title for this book! I'll think about that later, anyway. ...

I felt comfortable speaking. I was full of energy, making people laugh, and knew I was giving the audience a good presentation. It was wonderful having an audience who could relate to me when I was talking about the profession and growing up around death. I've created a six-minute video that I run during presentations, just in case some haven't watched the reality show. It capsulizes what I did on the show and how I handled everything, which helps getting questions started. I was curious what they were going to ask.

I spoke about an hour before the floor was opened to questions. It was so funny. Male funeral directors were asking more questions than the women. Yes, there tend to be more men in funeral services, but usually males aren't as interested in reality shows and drama as women! Well, this crowd was totally into it. We were all having a blast. The next speaker was scheduled to talk at 9:30 but we were running overtime because of all the questions. I had to stop, although hands were still raised. Many came up afterwards, asking more questions, taking photos of me with them, and requesting autographs.

The rest of the convention went well. I was pleasantly surprised with the early-bird turnout for my presentation. Oh, and we did visit Monterey Bay Aquarium. Great trip.

I have enjoyed all my speaking engagements and want more. I have a new passion along with the funeral profession. The best part is I've been able to incorporate the funeral industry into my speaking engagements about the show. I learned people (not just funeral directors) like hearing how I got into the profession as much as they enjoy hearing about the reality show.

A former professor asked if I would be willing to give some of his new mortuary students a tour. It was required they visit a funeral home. A lot of them wanted to visit Newton-Bracewell Chico Funeral Home. Yes, I would love to meet his new and upcoming students.

I like asking students why they're entering the funeral profession. Most pursue it because of a family owned funeral home and it seems like the right thing to do, or they went to a funeral of someone close and decided it was their calling to help the dead. Occasionally students will say, "I just want to work around dead people." They seldom make it through a semester.

The students on tour were mostly older than I, some had family in the business, and some saw it as a caring profession—an alternative to nursing. They wanted me to tell them about the mortuary program and how I got through microbiology and chemistry (among the hardest classes in the program). All I could say was … flash cards—flash cards and coffee. I suggested they try and work at a funeral home right away to get experience sooner than later. They said it was hard to get a funeral home job. I think it's just as hard, in general, to find any job.

I gave them the tour, like I do with the nursing students, only this time no one passed out on me. They handled the prep room as I hoped they would. Afterwards, they asked about the program, the boards, and state tests. It was nice conversing with future funeral directors.

There were more women than men, which is the trend for those entering the profession. They seem to have a natural ability to be caregivers and nurturers. Women embalmers are still rare. I love saying I am one of those rare ones.

Thinking back on these tours, speeches, and conventions I wonder how I found time and energy to work at the funeral home. Good question! The answer is I've learned to share my time with what I love. The reality show has led to many opportunities and experiences. There will be more.

I RECENTLY RECEIVED an invitation to be closing keynote speaker at a conference in Chico. Me … a keynote speaker? I was so excited I ran into my dad's office to tell him without finishing the email. He asked, "What's the conference about?" I looked like a deer caught in the headlights. I had no clue. "Ummm good question, let me find out." Sometimes I get a little too excited—obviously.

It was the inaugural Wondrous Women conference. Alicia, the Wondrous Women founder, teaches at Chico State. She started a blog of encouragement and topics for women to discuss. Her website became so popular she decided to expand. She wanted to create an all-women conference to inspire, encourage, and motivate women. I liked this idea and replied, "Let's meet."

Alicia is beautiful, young, and was going through a difficult divorce. She described her website inspiration not only for women going through a divorce, but anything and everything. I loved her openness because I, too, am a very open woman (hence I'm writing this book), and I began to tell her about my life and what has been going on with me.

I asked if the reason she invited me to speak was the reality show. She hadn't watched it but her friends suggested I come and talk about character building based on what they saw me go through on the show. I briefed her about it and how I remained a lady and kept my integrity. I told her about my job, what I learned from the difficult relationship with Lane, and previous speeches given to organizations.

The conference was heavily promoted thanks to sponsors, community support, and public service announcements. Over a hundred people bought tickets. Topics included following your dreams, how to handle your finances, self-defense, being your own voice, and mine—how I kept my own reality.

I spoke about being a funeral director at a young age and the impact the job has made on my life. I encouraged the audience not to ignore the little voice inside them. I reminded them to take risks—that's what makes life exciting. When I talked about the reality show I sensed their undivided attention. I concluded by describing my ability to handle my own reality not only on the show, but in life.

I shared the horrible things people said about me, my work, family, and even my looks and how difficult that was to ignore. I refrained from negativity and focused on the positives. My ending words were, "No matter who you are, even if you're Jesus Christ or Mother Theresa, people are still going to have something negative to say about you. It's how you handle that negativity that matters." I felt like I contributed to the purpose of the conference and even inspired myself to continue to stay clear from the negative and focus on what matters: the positive.

Afterwards, many approached and asked if I would speak to their class or association sometime. I was assured the audience left inspired and encouraged. We all need reassurance sometimes!

Now What?

My goodness, I think it's safe to say my life is now an open book! I have detailed my milestones: growing up in the funeral industry and, oh, how can we forget? my dating life.

Some of the stories about being a funeral director were difficult to write, yet I wanted to share them with you. I hope you received comfort from the stories, or could relate to the families from having a similar experience. I know I said this before, but it's important to repeat it: funeral directors try and work hard to help serve families during one of the most difficult times in their life. The average family makes about sixty-two decisions for the normal funeral service. Funeral directors are there to guide them in the right direction.

Being a funeral director has helped me become the woman I am today and I am grateful. Just to clarify, I am not saying everyone needs to enroll in mortuary school to become the person they are supposed to be. My goodness that would just be nuts. I'm just saying that I learned for myself that being a funeral director molded my character and enabled me to handle difficult situations. I have the ability to make families comfortable enough to feel safe and know they can trust and allow me to help them arrange a celebration.

The downside of being a funeral director, however, is it hasn't helped me much with my dating life. It definitely challenges my dating. I know, I know, I know, you were hoping I would conclude this book with a fairy-tail ending telling you I found my prince and am happily in love. Well, not yet! But I have hope and I know he's out there (maybe he's reading this book now and getting ready to come find me ... wishful thinking?!?!).

Words from a wise woman, my grandmother: "He'll find you when you least expect it."

JUST A FEW moments ago, as I'm finishing my conclusion of this book, I received a phone call from a friend who told me her little baby boy died. She was in tears. I could hardly understand her. Her son had health problems for months—doctors had been doing tests after tests after tests. Her little boy tired and did not make it.

You see how everything can change quickly with life and death—even for me? I was just sitting on the couch with my laptop, the phone rang, and I'm hearing my friend's voice quiver telling me she just said goodbye to her own child. I am sure you now have a feel for the life of a funeral director.

I believe many of us sometimes take life for granted and don't appreciate every breath we take. Being a woman of faith, I try and thank God every day for the life I have been given and the opportunities that have come my way. I know I am truly blessed and sometimes feel undeserving of all my blessings.

We all have God-given gifts and I encourage each and

every one of us to use those gifts, explore them, reach out, and take risks. Who knew I would ever be a funeral director/embalmer and go on some reality show for a couple months and come back to new doors that opened and are still opening? I took the risks, and I listened to that little voice inside of me.

Thank you for taking the time to hear my story. I hope and pray this book has brought you some comfort. As my grandpa would say, "Everybody happy, say *amen*." Well, Grandpa, Amen!!

Shawntel atop Mt. Lassen at 10,457-foot elevation

CPSIA information can be obtained at www.ICGtesting.com
Printed in the USA
LVOW101414100212

268121LV00006B/3/P